the 21st Century

a view from the South

Ricardo Lagos

56 Haymarket, London, SW1Y 4RN, UK.
Tel: +44 20 7389 9650 Fax: +44 20 7389 9644
Email: publisher@firstmagazine.com
URL: www.firstmagazine.com

First published in the United Kingdom by FIRST,
56 Haymarket, London, SW1Y 4RN, United Kingdom in 2005.

© Speech/article text: Ricardo Lagos 2005.
The right of Ricardo Lagos to be identified as the author of this work has been asserted by him in accordance with the Copyright, Designs and Patents Act 1988.
All rights reserved. No part of this publication may be reproduced, stored in a retrievable system, or transmitted, in any form or by any means without the prior permission in writing of the publisher, nor be otherwise circulated in any form of binding or cover other than that in which it is published and without a similar condition including this condition being imposed on the subsequent purchaser.

ISBN: 0-9546409-1-8

Printed in the United Kingdom.

© This edition FIRST 2005.
Initial translations from the original by the staff of the President's office.
This edition revised by the Editorial Department of FIRST.

The Publishers would like to acknowledge the assistance of the
Embassy of Chile, London.

FIRST

56 Haymarket, London, SW1Y 4RN, UK
Tel: +44 20 7389 9650 Fax: +44 20 7389 9644
E-mail: publisher@firstmagazine.com
Website: www.firstmagazine.com

Chairman Rupert Goodman,
Chief Operating Officer Eamonn Daly,
President Sir Patrick Cormack FSA MP,
Non Executive Directors Timothy Bunting, Hon. Alexander Hambro,
Head of Corporate Business Andrew Tweedie,
Executive Publisher Alastair Harris, **Regional Publisher** Colin Kilkelly,
Editorial Consultant Jonathan Gregson, **Production Manager** Rachel Dipper,
PA – Chairman's Office Lisa Harbron, **PA** Armelle Noyelle,
Secretariat Gil Pearson, **Design Consultant** Stanley Glazer,
Special Adviser, Russia Sir Andrew Wood GCMG,
Award Advisory Panel Lord Dahrendorf KBE, Rt Hon Lord Howe of Aberavon CH, QC, Hon Raymond Seitz, Lord Plant of Highfield, Chief Emeka Anyaoku, GCVO, TC, CFR, Lord Browne of Madingley, Marilyn Carlson Nelson, Sir Robert Wilson KCMG, Dr Daniel Vasella, Morris Tabaksblat KBE

ALL INFORMATION IN THIS PUBLICATION IS VERIFIED TO THE BEST OF THE AUTHORS AND PUBLISHERS' ABILITY, BUT NO RESPONSIBILITY CAN BE ACCEPTED FOR LOSS ARISING FROM DECISIONS BASED ON THIS MATERIAL, WHERE OPINION IS EXPRESSED IT IS THAT OF THE AUTHOR.

"In a democracy, being the President of the Republic is not a privilege. It is the exercise of a mandate bestowed by a sovereign people, to whom one is answerable each and every day."
RICARDO LAGOS

Contents

7
Foreword
Rt. Hon. Tony Blair MP, Prime Minister

9
Chile and its integration into the global world
Introductory article

Chile: Democracy and Progress

23
The rebirth of Chile
Excerpts from the speech at the Opening of the Congressional Year, Valparaiso, Chile, May 21st 2005

37
Building a country centred on the human being
Speech delivered on the presentation of the Rectorial Medal for the 50th Anniversary of his joining the Faculty of Law, University of Chile, Santiago, Chile, March 7th 2005

49
Chile's latest step on the path to truth
Article published in The Christian Science Monitor, Boston, United States of America, December 3rd 2004

53
Without democracy, there can be no progress
Excerpts from the speech to open the 3rd Ministerial Conference of the Community of Democracies, Santiago, Chile, April 28th 2005

59
Chile 30 years later : The legacy of a crushed dream: 'Never again'
Article published in the International Herald Tribune, New York, United States of America, September 11th 2003

Contents
continued

Europe, Latin America and the Caribbean: To renew the long standing relations

65
The EU, Latin America and the Caribbean: Ten areas for collaboration
Article published in El País, Madrid, Spain, July 9th 2002

69
2003 Canning Lecture: How this world is being organised?
Transcript of the lecture delivered on July 14th 2003 in Lancaster House, London, United Kingdom

81
The European-Southern Hemisphere relationship
Edited version of the speech delivered in the Progressive Governance Conference, Budapest, Hungary, October 14th 2004

91
Agreement of Political Association, Commerce and Cooperation Chile-EU
Speech on the occasion of the signing of the Agreement. Second Summit Conference of the European Union/ Latin America and the Caribbean, Madrid, Spain, May 17th, 2002

Security and Human Rights in the Globalised World

95
Getting back on the right track
Article published in El País-Internacional, Madrid, Spain, April 22nd 2003

Contents
continued

99
What is a utopia if it isn't our dream of a better world?
A message to students at the University of Duke, North Carolina, United States of America, May 15th 2005

109
Declaration for the release of Aung San Suu Kyi
Joint declaration by Ricardo Lagos, Thabo Mbeki, Göran Persson and Helen Clark, published in the International Herald Tribune, New York, United States of America, June 18th 2005

Development, Technology and Globalisation

113
Public goods and citizenship: How do we proceed?
Article published in El País, Madrid, Spain, September 5th 2003

117
The challenges to harness IT for the poor
Joint article by Ricardo Lagos, Thabo Mbeki and Göran Persson, published in the International Herald Tribune, New York, United States of America, July 14th 2000

121
A view from the South
Edited version of the speech delivered in the Round Table of the Progressive Governance Conference, London, United Kingdom, July 12th 2003. Participants included Bill Clinton, Ricardo Lagos, Jean Chretien, Pascal Lamy and Jack Straw.

New Partnerships across the World

129
Free Trade Agreement Chile-USA
Speech on the occasion of the signing of the Free Trade Agreement between Chile and the United States of America, Santiago, Chile, June 6th 2003

Contents
continued

133
Chile and South Africa: Ethical Bonds
Article published in Mail and Guardian, Johannesburg, South Africa, April 30th 2004

137
Chile and China look to the future
Article published on the occasion of the visit of President Hu Jintao to Chile and in commemoration of the APEC Chile year, in China Daily, Beijing, China, November 18th 2004

139
APEC and MERCOSUR:
An opportunity presents itself
Article published in Clarín, Buenos Aires, Argentina, August 30th 2004

143
We are a bridge to South America
Published in The Economic Times, New Dehli, India, January 19th 2005

Interviews

149
We need to live in a world that is much more secure
Interview in Public Broadcasting Service (PBS), Program "Commanding Heights", United States of America, January 19th 2002

177
Chile's socialist leader is betting on the New Economy
Interview in International Latin America Business Week, New York, United States of America, April 2nd 2001

Contents
continued

183
We worry about the recurrent crises
Interview in Weekly Report Latin American Newsletter, London, United Kingdom, August 13th 2002

189
Latin America after the Cold War
Interview in Magazine Polityka, Warsaw, Poland, October 12th 2002

195
We are planning... 5 per cent growth in GDP
Interview by Herbert Klein, editor-in-chief of Copley Newspapers, published in San Diego Union-Tribune and others, California, United States of America, April 20th 2003

203
Chilean model
Interview in monthly magazine ASIA INC, Singapore, Singapore, November 2004

211
There is no tomorrow without yesterday
Interview in the weekly magazine Al Ahram, Cairo, Egypt, April 14-20th 2005

221
The importance of dreaming about the future
Interview by Jose Zepeda Varas, Director of the Latin American Department of Radio Nederland, The Netherlands, April 4th 2005

231 - Place Index
235 - Personality Index
239 - Acronyms Index

Foreword by Tony Blair

Britain and Chile have always had an affinity. In the nineteenth century British sailors, merchants and engineers helped Chile first gain independence and then build a thriving national economy.

Many stayed on as immigrants, adding their British surnames to Chile's social melting pot. Today Britain and Chile confront similar challenges: how to ensure the future prosperity of our two globalised economies; how to build opportunity and justice in our two societies; and how to guarantee peace and security for our two peoples. I am delighted that Britain and Chile are working so closely together on this common agenda. No one has done more to make this happen than my friend Ricardo Lagos.

Ricardo Lagos has had a remarkable political career. A brilliant academic economist and socialist party sympathiser he caught the eye of Salvador Allende who wanted to use him for various important diplomatic missions. After spending several years, in the US, he was able to return to Chile in 1978 to work for various international organisations based in Santiago. On the restoration of democratic rule at the end of the 1980s he became one of the major figures in the centre-left coalition that has held power since 1990.

In 2000 he took office as the first Socialist President of Chile since Allende. Under his Presidency Chile has further consolidated its democratic credentials and continued on the path of economic development. Chile is now recognised as one of the most prosperous and politically stable countries in Latin America. While adhering to the basic principles of a free market economy President Lagos has put in place social programmes which have made an impressive impact on poverty levels, now among the lowest in the region. At the same time he has worked to heal the divisions in a society where the traumas of the past are now being finally laid to rest.

The speeches, articles and interviews gathered in this book, and published for the first time in English, set out some of the theoretical thinking behind these remarkable achievements. I commend this book to anyone who is interested in how the values inherited from socialism can be applied in a 21st century society.

Chile and its integration into the global world *

WHEN I TOOK office on March 11th 2000, I did so as the first Chilean President of the twenty-first century. I was aware from the very beginning that one of my key tasks would be to take the measure of the changes brought by the new century and of the transformations taking place in our world. Understanding those changes would, I realised, be vital for the success of Chile's integration into the global world that was emerging before our eyes.

As my term of office now draws to a close, it is appropriate to look back at the road which we have travelled and the lessons we have learned.

There are those - such as Eric Hobsbawm - who argue that this century actually started before 2000, with the end of the Cold War and the great changes it brought in the balance of world power. And, in the 1990s, a number of important summits - such as the Río Summit of 1992 on the environment and the Copenhagen Summit of 1995 on social development - were already helping to shape a new international agenda. In these and other meetings, both governments and civil society, represented by NGOs, were anticipating the challenges that would exercise contemporary political thought at both a local and international level.

The world today is very different from that of just twenty years ago when, in Chile, we were struggling to reinstate democracy. A world with today's capacity for instant communication is very different from a world without the Internet. The concept of the

---

* *Introductory article written by Ricardo Lagos especially for this book.*

nation state that developed in the twentieth century, or even before, is not the same as the concept of a state in today's interdependent world. A nation is not the same as a country. Scientific knowledge, when used to benefit humanity, is not the same as scientific knowledge, when used as an instrument of power. Globalisation and market access are not the same for some, particularly in the northern hemisphere, as they are for others in the southern hemisphere.

Today, it is no longer only the state that represents a country internationally. Together with the meetings of presidents and prime ministers, or foreign ministers and other government officials, we see political leaders, business people and social movements holding their own international meetings and defining their own agendas. The World Economic Forum, which meets each year in Davos, Switzerland and the World Social Forum, which first met in Porto Alegre, Brazil in 2001, are just two examples of such contributions to the shaping of today's international agenda.

Our citizens - the people who must be the focus of our policies - see a world that has become more interconnected and more complex. And, in response, they are looking beyond their own borders - in a way that has never occurred before - to form associations with like-minded people around the world.

Four crucial questions

When I was sworn in as President, I knew it would be my job to find the answer to four crucial questions for the future of my country and its place in the world. How could we achieve a greater role for Chile, a small country, in a global world? How could we, along with others, help to ensure greater balance and fairer rules in the new international order that was emerging? How could we ensure that human beings would be at the centre of the process of globalisation, fostering both economic growth and social justice? And how could we contribute to the recognition of cultural diversity as part of the wealth of our planet?

The answer to the first of those questions is perhaps best

reflected in the free trade agreements that have improved Chile's access to some of the world's main markets. And, in various international organisations, we have borne witness to our belief that multilateralism is the best way to address the challenges of globalisation. In a bid to ensure that globalisation has a human face, we have supported the development of global public goods. And our commitment to cultural diversity is anchored in Chile's own experience of respect for ethnic minorities and the coexistence of peoples from different cultural origins.

In March 2000, there were two main concerns about the course my government would take. On the one hand, there were those who were wondering how a President from the left of the political spectrum would manage an economy in which the free market plays a very important role. And, on the other, there were others who were calling for justice for the victims of the human rights violations of the past and were wondering what we would be able to achieve in this field.

We set out to show that, in this new century, being a President with progressive convictions means being able to create the economic conditions required for growth. It is only through growth, responsible economic management, investment and saving, that it is possible to generate the resources to finance public policies that benefit those who are most under-privileged.

We also set out to show that our task today is to strengthen democracy and to create societies that are more just, more equal, more free, in which opportunities are open to all and in which respect for human rights is an inseparable part of a country's way of life. In Chile, after a very difficult period in our history, we believed that the road to the future lay through truth. It was our belief that if we were to face the future with confidence, we could not ignore the truth of the past, however terrible.

Particularly in the twentieth century, equality and liberty were seen as opposing forces, but today that is no longer acceptable. The road to equality is through democracy and public policies that aim to reduce differences. Liberty exists only when our citizens feel that society offers them the chance to realise their hopes and dreams.

On these essential issues, the men and women of Chile are no different from those of other countries. They seek answers on employment, healthcare, education and access to housing. They seek social protection provided by systems that are caring, efficient and comprehensive. The ways in which these goals are achieved may differ, but the goals themselves are similar.

Chile made a choice. It decided to become an open country and to seek growth and social development through international integration. That is why we have signed free trade agreements with the European Union, the United States and South Korea, among other countries, and why we are now working towards agreements with China and India.

By 2005, 73 per cent of Chile's GDP is related to international trade in goods and services, with exports representing 41 per cent and imports 32 per cent. In 2002, the Chilean economy grew by 2.2 per cent but, in 2005, it is set to expand by around 6 per cent. This is Chile's platform for growth, the platform from which, within a few years, we hope to join the ranks of the developed countries.

We are aware that achieving this goal will depend primarily on Chile itself and will require political resolve. In the longer term, populism is never the right answer. That belief was reflected in Chile's decision as from 2000 to maintain a structural fiscal surplus equivalent to 1% of GDP. We have worked to keep our economy in order and to achieve international credibility. That explains why, as of August 2005, Chile's country-risk was running at just 52 points, one of the lowest levels seen among the world's emerging economies.

When a country goes out to compete in today's world, it does so on the basis of all that it represents, its growth and development, the coherence of its goals and policies, the quality of its democracy and the strength of its cultural roots. But we have also learned that competing internationally is not an easy task if the world lacks rules which are clear and fair for all. Chile has insisted - vehemently at times - on the need for shared norms because much of our country's future depends on the existence of such rules.

Chile and its integration into the global world

CHILE'S POLICY FRAMEWORK

The government coalition - Concertación de Partidos por la Democracia - first took office in 1990 under President Patricio Aylwin. It embarked on the task of rebuilding Chile's democracy just as sweeping changes were taking place in the world. The balance of power that dated back to the Peace of Westphalia was breaking down with the end of the Cold War and the emergence of a bipolar world order.

As Chile sought to lay to rest a past - on which the Cold War had also left its mark - it had to do so in the context of a world in which new maps were being drawn, new conflicts were emerging and the consequences of globalisation were becoming increasingly apparent. It was also against this background that President Eduardo Frei continued the task of identifying new global opportunities for Chile.

When I took my place in the La Moneda Palace, the seat of Chile's Presidents, the world was still grappling with its surprise at the protests that had paralysed the World Trade Organisation conference in Seattle, and the questions they had raised. One issue dominated international debate - globalisation - and that was part of the context in which my administration would govern.

Were two new poles emerging around the issue of globalisation? On the one hand, its supporters and, on the other, its detractors? Were we to take globalisation, with its consequences and its deficiencies, as the foundation on which to build a new international order compatible with the shape the world was taking? Was globalisation itself sufficient, or was it also necessary - precisely because of globalisation - to reinforce the world's multilateral organisations?

In my first State of the Nation Message in May 2000, I spoke of my optimism in the face of this task: "we live in a new century and I believe we are at the dawn of a new age. On every side, we see new energy, new ways of working and of communicating, of living and of doing business. Chile must play a pre-eminent role in the global world that is emerging before our eyes." And I also underlined the importance of "looking to the future while, at the same time, learning from the past".

My experience as President has confirmed my view that there are two essential requirements for dealing with today's global world: to follow the form the world is taking and the way in which it works very closely and, secondly, to consolidate a country's identity and its values as the basis for international insertion.

As regards the first, we do not want to live on a planet in which there are those who "globalise" and others who "are globalised", where there are those who set the rules and others who simply have to adhere to them. We want a form of international coexistence that is grounded in clear rules. In the struggle to achieve this end, it is essential, especially for a small country like Chile, to join forces with others, reinforcing a shared vision.

Globalisation was already at the centre of international debate when, in September 2001, another issue came violently to the fore - terrorism. It is these two issues that have marked the start of this century, leading us down previously unexplored paths politically, economically, socially and culturally.

At a national level, public goods have evolved, bringing with them progress towards greater equity, but they are also evolving internationally. Just forty or fifty years ago, the environment was not prominent on the international agenda. Similarly, human rights have expanded beyond the protection of life and social development to include third and fourth generation concepts. And this evolution will continue to gather speed, demanding new answers from us.

In the view of many people, the market plays the key role in the world today. They argue that the market drives our economies and our social relations. The market is, of course, essential in assigning resources, both nationally and globally. The outsourcing adopted by many firms, in order to reduce costs and focus on their core business, is just one example of the market's global reach. But the market also has limitations. As President, I have more than once stated that I believe in the market economy, but not in the market society. The market, I have insisted, is a place for consumers, not citizens. The power of consumers is measured in terms of income, while the power of citizens is measured by the votes which they cast.

It is our citizens who, through the processes of democracy, determine the thrust and priorities of public policies. And, although it is the state that draws up these policies, they can be implemented either by the public or private sector.

But what does it mean to be a citizen today? That is a question to which the leaders of the modern world do not have an easy answer. Participation in public affairs through the right to vote is at the root of the concept of citizenship. Historically, that right was restricted but, through persistent struggle, those who were excluded for reasons of race, economic status or gender, gradually achieved enfranchisement. The twentieth century saw an expansion of the democratic and social state and of citizenship, and we understood that the latter not only involves civil and political rights, but also economic, social, cultural and environmental rights. And, by the same token, it also entails a duty to participate in public life.

Now, as well as fostering social cohesion and strengthening democracy, we face another challenge - that of guaranteeing the right of citizenship in a world that is ever more integrated, ever more global and ever more demanding, and in which cultural diversity plays a central role.

Towards global public goods

On September 11, 2001, I was in Lisbon at the time of the terrorist attacks in New York and Washington. When I arrived in London later the same day, it was already clear that the world had changed. Looking back, I believe those events contained the seed of an opportunity of which we have yet to take advantage. Faced with terrorism - and the subsequent attacks such as occurred in Bali, Madrid and, most recently, London - the international community has had a great opportunity to embark on a new stage of international cooperation. It has an opportunity to create a new model of dialogue and new rules tailored to the realities of the twenty-first century.

If we look back at history, we see that this is what happened at other times of crisis. The Treaty of Versailles - as well as its other consequences - created the League of Nations in a bid to build a better and more peaceful world from the ruins of the First World War. This was the context in which President Woodrow Wilson presented his Fourteen Points. And then, in 1945, at the end of the Second World War, the United Nations was created in an attempt to establish a more solid system of international relations, with broader objectives, that would give the world stability.

But that is not what has happened recently in response to terrorism. The largest coalition ever formed around a single political issue said NO to terrorism, but that was not accompanied by the corresponding YES to cooperation and the construction of a world anchored in rules that are clear, fair and balanced.

We may understand why it has not happened, but that does not make it acceptable. What we have seen in the intervening years is an increasing contradiction between two features of today's world - globalisation and multilateralism. Globalisation is gaining in strength, but multilateralism is failing to advance.

That is not good either for the world, as a whole, or for its powers, whether they be the G7 countries or vast multinational corporations. Even a unipolar world, such as exists today, cannot be shaped by a single power in the absence of dialogue with other countries. Moreover, for a country like Chile, with just 15 million inhabitants and a medium level of development, multilateralism and shared norms are crucial for providing the necessary mutual guarantees.

If we fail to understand this aspect of multilateralism, we will not have grasped the logic of the contemporary world.

I have made this point many times in Latin America because our region is the basis from which Chile seeks to build its foreign policy. Let us imagine for a moment that the majority of Latin American countries are implementing policies that combine economic growth with a strong emphasis on social needs. Let us also imagine a region in which integration and social development go hand-in-hand. But that would still not address the main challenge - that of creating norms for a world in which globalisation crosses all frontiers.

In 1945, the United Nations was set up to create a multilateral system with norms to resolve differences and to achieve progress. But what is happening today? Are we going to have policies that increase the availability of the so-called public goods, such as protection of the environment, international justice, human rights and the fight against poverty, hunger and world epidemics? How are we going to foster cultural diversity, human knowledge and the use of common goods? How far will we be able to advance in creating norms to regulate international economic transactions, the world macroeconomy and financial stability?

As the world becomes more global, the concept of global public goods is gaining ground. The need for such goods is becoming more evident, especially when we talk about new citizen's rights.

In Punta Arenas in the far south of Chile, when our schoolchildren go out to play on a sunny day, they have to use special protection from its rays. That is the result of a thinning of the ozone layer caused by gas emissions in the northern hemisphere. The question is to whom we can or should complain about this threat to the health of our children.

Some countries do not like the Kyoto Protocol and they are entitled to their view. However, the central question remains. How can we address the problem of the citizens of Punta Arenas? The remedy is, after all, not in Chile's hands, but depends on an agreement between many countries.

MULTILATERALISM AND DOMESTIC POLICIES

This takes us to another of the fundamental lessons of our time - that multilateralism must increasingly be a feature of our domestic policies.

If anti-dumping measures - with which Chile is not in agreement and hopes, together with others, to change - are applied to our products, the effects are felt in very specific areas of our country. When, for example, Chilean salmon is denied access to a particular market that means unemployment in the south of Chile. And we have to explain to those who are out of work that the crisis is the result of events outside Chile about which we can do very little because there is still not a place where we can go to defend our interests. It is in such cases that the importance of the multilateral arena as the logical place to discuss our differences becomes so evident.

At the heart of the multilateral challenge is the need to define what we understand as global public goods and to create the conditions in which they can exist and grow. If each individual country identifies education, healthcare, housing and infrastructure as among the public goods that should be available to all, then it is logical to aspire to public policies that also guarantee these goods on a global scale.

This means that governance on a global scale - understood as the logical extension of the institutional order that each state has established - can only be achieved if the interests of all, not just the few, are represented. History teaches us that, in the absence of shared rules, it is the interests of the strongest that prevail.

That is the underlying reason why, as a member of the United Nations Security Council between 2003 and 2004, Chile understood that its first duty was to strengthen multilateral institutions. Our experience there confirmed our belief in the need for decisive joint action, backed with the necessary legitimacy. As we then told the President of the United States, we were not in agreement with the way in which the crisis in Iraq evolved. For a country like Chile, it was not easy to take such a stance. However, we believed that the essential values of our country and its principle-based policies were at stake.

It was those same principles we put into practice when faced with the crisis in Haiti. In just 72 hours, Chile placed 300 soldiers in Haiti. That was what our principles dictated in the face of the Security Council's unanimous request for assistance - the more so because, in this case, the crisis occurred in a fellow Latin American country, afflicted by chaos and poverty.

Chile and its integration into the global world

The world needs the United Nations. However, it is also important to recognise that today's multilateral system has its origins not in the world of 2005, but in the world of 1945, when the San Francisco Charter was signed. The creation of multilateral institutions in accordance with the needs of today's world and its emerging global realities is the key challenge of our time.

It is also important to remember that it is not only relations between states that have changed. We have also seen a profound transformation of economic relations on a global scale. To understand the magnitude of this transformation, it is worth looking at the trillions of dollars in international financial flows that are now transferred at the touch of a button through digital networks, or at the enormous influence that country-risk classification agencies now have. The organisations that were created as a result of the Bretton Woods Conference of 1944 were not designed for today's world and its dynamic economy. The lack of appropriate rules affects the material future of the citizens of the world today.

Some countries still need help to emerge from under-development; others, like Chile, need fair trade to allow them to compete in order to grow. Those countries that were victorious in 1945 acquired special benefits to lead the world. Others have grown into a position of influence as their development and international credibility have increased.

In other words, if we want social cohesion as an essential feature of our countries, how much social cohesion are we going to have on a global scale in a multilateral system? We are convinced that it is our ethical duty to advance in this direction.

These are the issues on which this book seeks to throw some light. It brings together interviews, opinions and articles that - in one way or another - are part of a political record of my aims and experiences as President of Chile.

It is my firm belief that change is vital in order to give a new form to public policies at both a national and global level, placing human beings at their centre. Globalisation without social cohesion is a dangerous road. It is not the road we should take. We should follow the signposts of equity.

Chapter 1

Chile:
Democracy and Progress

The rebirth of Chile *

TODAY, AT THE start of this twenty-first century, Chile is a stronger and different country.

It is a country that believes in and practises democracy, republicanism, liberty and pluralism.

Today, Chile strictly adheres to the principle of respect for human rights - those of today, of tomorrow and of yesterday.

Today, Chileans enjoy a degree of personal freedom - freedom of thought and expression, freedom to create and forge their own destiny - that is without precedent in our country's history. Today, Chile's outlook is broader; Chile can see things it did not see before, and its horizons have widened.

We have entered the world by the front door. Chile is a country that has opened its borders, that has economic, political and cultural relations with the rest of the world. It is admired and respected in all corners of the earth.

Today, Chile has an economy that is growing, and is doing so solidly.

Today, Chile is winning the war on poverty and there are irrefutable signs of improvement in social justice, in the distribution of opportunities, in education and healthcare, in the workplace and in access to goods and services.

Spectacular infrastructure development has brought highways, ports, airports and telecommunications services that put us on a par with the developed world.

But, above all, Chile is today a country that is wiser and more mature, a country that has learned to believe in itself. It is a coun-

---

Excerpts from the speech at the Opening of the Congressional Year, Valparaiso, Chile, May 21st 2005

try that can look with pride at what has been achieved through joint endeavour, and a country that is eager to continue building a better future for all its men and women.

Today, Chile's 15 million inhabitants are the drivers of change.

As we enter this twenty-first century, we are seeking to promote further progress for Chile.

At the turn of this century, Chile's men and women have channelled their dreams and hopes down a path of sustained progress along which we are advancing step-by-step, without demagoguery, without false rhetoric and without populism, but moving steadily towards our goals. In this twenty-first century, Chile is no longer - nor will be - a case of frustrated development as, in the words of Aníbal Pinto, it was at the turn of the last century. Chile is, and will be, an example of a country that is achieving successful development and in which the benefits of growth and development are shared by all its citizens in every corner of the country.

RENEWED GROWTH

Yes, Chile is firmly back on the road of growth. Today, we can claim high, solid and sustainable growth because, in the lean years, we adopted the right policies. In 2004, the economy expanded by 6.1 per cent and will grow by around 6 per cent, or slightly more, this year. Today, Chile's gross domestic product is 21 per cent larger than in 1999.

Manufacturing, commerce, services, agriculture and mining are all growing. The value of our agricultural exports has increased by an average 11 per cent annually over the last five years. Our state copper company, Codelco, has doubled its value and, over the past year, has generated more than US$3.3 billion in profits. Investment in mining is booming. At the same time, we have introduced a royalty on mining, and I would like to thank Congress for its approval of that bill.

If Chile is to continue growing, we need strong investment in innovation, science and technology. Although spending on research and development has increased fourfold in the last decade, it is still below the level seen in the world's most developed and innovative countries. By the end of my administration, we will be investing between 1 per cent and 1.2 per cent of GDP in research and development. In developed countries, that figure averages 2.1 per cent and, in the most innovative countries, is over 3 per cent.

In Chile, the private sector finances only 28 per cent of investment in research and development whereas, in developed countries, it finances 68 per cent.

Chile can and must aim to devote at least 1.5 per cent of GDP to research and development by 2010, and half of that investment should come from the private sector. The recent approval of the Royalty Law is a decisive step in the creation of an Innovation Fund. That Fund is a legacy we want to leave for future generations.

It is the seed of future development. From the foundations that we have laid, Chile will be able to advance towards new goals like an athlete, who must beat his or her own previous record before moving on to more ambitious targets.

In 2004, Chile's country risk reached its lowest level ever and is, of course, the lowest among our fellow Latin American countries. When Chile announced that it would maintain a 1 per cent structural fiscal surplus, that decision was not understood by many and its full significance was not appreciated. Today, however, the results are there for all to see in terms of international confidence, economic performance and, particularly, social development. It was thanks to this decision that, in the lean years, we could maintain a high level of social spending. What a difference from the past when, in a crisis, social spending was the first to be cut! We no longer need to resort to such cuts.

Today, Chile is the most competitive economy of the region, the country with the least corruption, the country with the most efficient public services, the country that is the leader in human development in Latin America.

We have, as a result, every right to look to the future with optimism, paying no heed to outdated prophecies of gloom. Our efforts to associate ourselves with the world's main economies are already bearing fruit. Between 2000 and 2004, Chile's exports rose by 76 per cent. Investment has increased by more than 12 per cent in the past year and, today, reaches 25 per cent of GDP, while consumer spending has risen by 5.6 per cent.

Those figures are a sign of a sustained effort, of entrepreneurship and of confidence. They are the foundations on which the people of Chile want to continue building their future...

TOWARDS GREATER EQUITY

As we have said before - and will not tire of repeating - growth only makes sense if it means greater wellbeing for all Chileans.

Our political vocation is a vocation for equality. That has always been so, and it is the reason for our efforts to reform education, healthcare, the civil courts and labour tribunals, to create jobs, and to achieve international integration.

There are those who, for years, have insisted that economic growth automatically leads to social justice. How wrong they are to wait for the so-called trickle-down effect! The market differentiates and discriminates according to how much each individual has to spend on consumption. Equity and social justice require political will; they require the design and implementation of realistic public policies so as to ensure that the benefits of growth are shared by all Chilean families.

This is the essence of our work as a government...

DEMOCRATIC INSTITUTIONS

Chile is achieving full democracy as it improves its freedoms and culture. The recovery of democracy required persistence, but the efforts of the different governments that have held office since 1990 are now close to bearing fruit.

The Senate has already passed - and the Chamber of Deputies has all but approved - a reform of Chile's constitution that will bring it into line with the basic requirements of full democracy. I would like to thank solemnly all the members of this National Congress for this historic step. Only one modification is still pending, and I hope it will soon pass the Chamber of Deputies.

We have taken this step because we needed to improve the quality of our democracy. In this field, four other very important bills should also become law this year. These will increase the powers of the Financial Analysis Unit, set up to prevent money laundering, regulate campaign financing in presidential elections and place a cap on spending, regulate lobbying, and oblige government authorities to disclose their assets.

I believe that these four bills are of fundamental importance. Today, our Armed Forces are once again the Armed Forces of all Chileans, and are once again an integral part of our country's democratic life. They are dedicated entirely to their professional role in defence, they participate actively in the task of national development, and they perform outstandingly in international missions, thereby collaborating efficiently in the implementation of Chile's foreign policy...

HUMAN RIGHTS

In the recovery of our historical memory, the quest for truth and justice necessarily played a vital role.

I think we can say with pride that, of all the countries that have suffered massive violations of human rights such as we have experienced, very few have shown the sustained progress that Chile has achieved in a process that began under President Aylwin with the Rettig Commission, continued under President Frei with the Roundtable Dialogue, and culminated with the Report on Torture published last year. On behalf of all Chileans, I would like to thank Monsignor Valech and the Commission over which he presided for their work in uncovering the truth, a task they undertook with great patriotism and little regard for the personal cost.

In 2005, the victims of torture, identified in the Report of the National Commission on Political Detention and Torture, will receive the reparation benefits that we announced last year, and we will create - with the support of this National Congress, I am sure – the National Institute for Human Rights.

By recovering our collective memory, facing up to the truth of what happened, and taking responsibility for the past, we have become a nation that is stronger, more mature and better able to harness the efforts of all Chileans to the task of building our country's future. That was our goal...

CULTURE

Today, Chile is not only a more democratic society. It is also more pluralistic, more diverse and more tolerant. Its outlook has broadened, and it is eager to learn about the progress that humanity is achieving in so many different spheres.

That is why we have been able to look back at our painful past. That is why women now play an outstanding role in practically every area of our national life. That is why we are paying more attention to the different regions, towns and cities that make up our country. That is why almost 15 million hectares of Chile - 19 per cent of our national territory - are protected natural reserves. And I am proud to say that, in these past five years, we have added 1.5 million hectares to that natural heritage or, in other words, a further 10 per cent in just five years.

That is also why, today, we have a new relationship with our native peoples. In education, we have created more than 150,000 scholarships for indigenous students. And, with regard to land, we have transferred over 260,000 hectares to indigenous communities.

As a society, we have a broader, more mature outlook and, in this context, protection of the environment and respect for our native peoples have a key place, and these are issues that we are learning to address collectively.

We see our country differently, taking a more modern, diverse and pluralistic view. And, because of this, Chile today is a society that is culturally richer.

The rebirth of Chile

As regards cultural activity, Chile is also integrated with the rest of the world and, through this exchange, reaffirms its own identity. We are both patriotic and universal and, through this dialogue with universal culture, Chile's own culture is further strengthened. Culture is what gives us identity. It is, in the end, culture that endures, that is the hallmark of a country.

Governments - and presidents - come and go. It is the work of artists that endures and gives identity to a country and, in Chile, this is demonstrated in the verse of our two Nobel poets, Gabriela Mistral and Pablo Neruda.

We have, then, brought about an enormous cultural change and, in this field, as in others, we are witnessing a transformation of our outlook.

A few examples serve to illustrate this change. We have abolished the death penalty. Film censorship was unacceptable and that has also been abolished. We have changed the law to eliminate the difference in the legal status of legitimate and illegitimate children. We have created a system of justice for minors. We have legalised divorce. We have implemented birth control policies and, in schools, we have ended discrimination against pregnant pupils.

In other words, my friends, we have put an end to anachronisms that seriously curtailed the freedom of Chileans.

Today, we are breathing new air, that of democracy and liberty…

INTERNATIONAL RELATIONS

As we have always stressed, Latin America is our great homeland, and the basis from which we conduct our foreign policy.

In today's globalised world, we believe that the time has come in which the peoples of the Americas should speak with one voice. The time has come in which the Organisation of American States should become the place where our countries can discuss their common problems, adopt common positions, or define the areas in which they differ, in the face of the challenges posed by globalisation.

We have a vision of America and its future. That is why Chile put forward one of its leading politicians, José Miguel Insulza, to lead this process of modernisation in the OAS.

In doing so, Chile demonstrated its maturity as a country. All Chileans, independent of their political allegiance, supported his candidacy. I would like to draw attention to this attitude and express my appreciation for it.

It is in this context that Chile's participation in efforts to establish and maintain peace in Haiti should be understood. And it is also in this context that we have played an active role in the Working Group against Hunger, an initiative that we launched together with Brazil's President Lula and France's President Chirac, and which Spain's President Rodríguez Zapatero and Germany's Chancellor Gerhard Schröder, have recently joined.

We are continuing to do our utmost to strengthen Chile's relations with its neighbours, seeking to negotiate a free trade agreement with Peru and to promote regional infrastructural integration with Brazil and Argentina.

Chile's free trade agreements with Europe, the United States and South Korea have, as we are all aware, been highly beneficial for our country. And, on the same lines, we are on the verge of completing a free trade agreement with New Zealand, Singapore and Brunei. We are also in the process of negotiating agreements with important emerging economies in Asia, such as China and India, and we have started talks with Japan.

What happens in the rest of the world has an enormous impact on Chile. The distinction between multilateral and local issues is becoming increasingly blurred and important multilateral events significantly effect Chile. What we have traditionally viewed as international or external issues are increasingly factors influencing our own domestic decisions. That is the way of today's world, and it will also be the way of the world of tomorrow.

Who assesses our performance when country risk is discussed in ratings agencies outside Chile? How much does it affect us if the developed countries decide to combat unemployment, or take austerity measures and opt to decrease their growth rates? Where, except in a multilateral organisation, can we discuss our needs as regards fair foreign trade? How can we influence those huge international forums unless we do so in the company of similar countries and speak with a single voice? This is the world of today, and it will also be the world of tomorrow. International factors have become crucial for our national development strategy and we must take these new parameters into account in drawing up our foreign and defence policies.

ONGOING PROGRESS FOR CHILE

Honourable members of Congress, we are laying the foundations for ongoing progress in Chile. Let me take a moment to look at the significance of what we have achieved, of what we are achieving, and of the principles that are the basis of our sense of dignity and progress.

What we are doing, what we have done, and what we will continue to do, has a long-term logic. We have governed from a perspective that is rooted in our past, in the profound lessons of our Republican history, but that also looks to the future, to 2010 when Chile will celebrate two hundred years of independence, and far beyond. We are, of course, building on the progress that was achieved under the democratic governments that preceded this administration. Chile today has a clearer vision of its future because we stand on the shoulders of those who came before. Our actions are motivated by a concept of Chile, of its history, its present and its future. We are inspired by a vision of the road that Chile can and must take - the road of progress and dignity for all its inhabitants.

We believe that our road to development requires simultaneous reforms on the economic, political, social and cultural fronts.

We - the great majority of Chileans - do not believe in a Chile forged in the image and likeness of the market because, if that were the case, our society would reproduce the inequalities of the market.

The market is made up of consumers, with unequal purchasing power, whereas society and democracy are made up of citizens, who are equal in their rights and obligations.

Why have we insisted, from the very beginning, that democracy had to be fully reflected in our country's constitution? That is because we are convinced that progress consists in ever increasing freedom, access to opportunities and citizen rights. Progressive dictatorships do not exist. Without democracy, there can be no progress.

Democracy is, ultimately, the way in which a country's citizens decide which public goods should be guaranteed to all, and the extent to which they should be made available. This is the key debate of the modern world.

We have placed so much emphasis on the growth of our economy because we are convinced that economic growth is a necessary condition for achieving solid improvements in the living standards of the underprivileged.

The supposed choice between growth and distribution is a false dilemma. Growth without distribution, or distribution without growth, inevitably leads to social and political crises and, in the last resort, to the loss of freedom. The only responsible and lasting way to achieve social progress is to improve distribution as the economy grows.

According to some, the maintenance of the existing model is all that is required to put this into practice. What a grave mistake! What a profound error! We are building a model of development that is based on democracy, on liberty, on the progressive inclusion of everyone in the benefits of growth, and on an unfailing respect for human rights.

Yes. This is a new concept, a new idea, a new way of understanding progress in a society whose axis is human dignity in all its dimensions.

The true measure of progress is the improvement in the quality of life of those who are poorest. Look around at Latin America. What has happened to the poorest 20 per cent of the population of our region? Look at what has happened to their income, but also to their access to housing, education and healthcare, and their participation in collective decisions. We are proud of what we have achieved.

Why did we choose this path? We did so because we seek progress for all, and the road to progress is constantly changing. At each step, we have to build new understandings and new majorities. The new world is not the result of an abrupt change; it does not take form overnight. It takes form gradually each and every day, like a tree that grows branch by branch, leaf by leaf.

There is no fast track that can replace our daily endeavours to reach new agreements that will allow us to expand the opportunities, rights and liberties of all our citizens.

When we say that democracy is the way in which public goods are made available to all citizens, it is because this is the result of public policy decisions and, as we grow, we see that we can give more and more to each one of our fellow Chileans.

And why, without abandoning our beliefs, have we put so much emphasis on international integration? This reflects our conviction that economic growth and cultural enrichment are the result of being open to the rest of the world, not of turning away from it. Countries such as ours - relatively small countries - need large markets if they are to progress. Similarly, the development of cultural identity can only be achieved through dialogue, or even debate, with other cultures. Isolation is anathema to progress. Isolationists and fundamentalists are the enemies of progress. They reject dialogue and the views of others; they fear the diversity that is to be found in others.

Why, then, has Chile attempted to recover its historical memory? In recent decades, our country - like other countries in our region - lived through extremes of horror, violence and hatred and, as we turn our eyes to the future, we are often tempted to simply forget and turn over the page.

But, if we are to progress, we must learn the lessons of that experience. The future must be built on strong moral foundations, and justice is a key element of those foundations. That is why, in Chile, we have said that there is no future without a past and that, if we are never again to live through such events, we must start by never again denying them.

That is a fundamental element in the philosophy that has inspired my government and also, I am proud to say, the Armed Forces in this democratic Chile.

Our vision of Chile's future means that we must proceed step by step. We value solid and lasting progress, rather than haste. We seek sensible agreements, not decisions imposed by force. We do not want to sacrifice social peace on the altar of justice but, by the same token, we are not willing to forego justice for the sake of an established order that benefits only a minority. As a great philosopher once said, we do not want conflict at any price, but nor do we want agreement at any price.

CONCLUDING REMARKS

My fellow Chileans, I have travelled the length and breadth of Chile. I have visited all the corners of my country. In so many homes, streets and town squares, all over Chile, I have been met and received with affection. That affection moves me deeply.

It reinforces my conviction that this concept of Chile, of its past and its future, this vision of new progress for our country, reflects the deepest hopes and dreams of all Chilean men and women. My duty is to them, and it is on their behalf that I work without flagging.

In a democracy, being the President of the Republic is not a privilege. It is the exercise of a mandate bestowed by a sovereign people, to whom one is answerable each and every day.

The dreams of a nation are not static. They change constantly, and interpreting them requires permanent, direct and frank communication. Direct and frank communication with the real authority: the people.

During my term of office, I have tried to listen, to discuss proposals and to exchange ideas with my fellow citizens every single day. That is the way in which I can best represent Chile.

The real privilege of being President is not being elected or wearing the ceremonial sash. It is the opportunity to be in close touch with the country, with the deepest corners of the country's soul.

Since taking office, I have become increasingly aware of this privilege, of this special contact with my people. And I have tried to interpret the hopes and dreams that Chile holds in its soul.

The opportunity for this contact with a society that is experiencing rapid and complex changes - which, in turn, trigger new hopes and anxieties - has moved me greatly, and fills me with gratitude.

That is why, today, I give thanks to Chile, and to history for allowing me to be a Chilean, accompanied by the 15 million Chilean men and women of today. As President, with their support, I have been able to interpret what they see as a definitive step from one era into another. Yes, my friends, from one era into another.

I am convinced of this.

I made my decision to enter politics at a time when the challenge was to, transform into reality, the words of our National Anthem: Chile, the land of the free, a refuge against oppression.

Chile is, at last, once again a land of freedom. Never again will it be a land of oppression.

Building a country centred on the human being *

DEMOCRACY cannot be protected with limitations. It can be protected with independent and educated citizens in charge of their own lives and who are active participants in the political process of the country. It was thanks to democracy that a former student of this Faculty reached the Presidency of the Republic as many of my predecessors have done.

However, I would also like to say that this former student hopes to leave the Presidency having obtained approval for the constitutional reforms needed for a better and fuller democracy. I trust that this will be possible. Fifty years ago, both the world and Chile was a very different place. So let us look back fifty years.

The world that existed in 1955 was a world very different to today's. It was different in its international structure, in its capacities and technological capabilities, in its relations between people, in the structure of society and in Chile's links with the world. Nevertheless, I believe that there is a strong, powerful and solid thread, which ties the ideals of today and those of 50 years ago.

The international situation then was marked by the Cold War, which was imposed after a brief consensual interregnum following World War II. And its defining mark was the division between antagonistic ideological blocks, which assumed the existence of separate worlds, of different and irreconcilable realities.

In 1948 the the Spanish sociologist José Medina Echavarría

---

* *Speech delivered on the presentation of the Rectorial Medal for the 50th Anniversary of his joining the Faculty of Law, University of Chile, Santiago, Chile, March 7th 2005* stated "a situation arises similar to the long-standing social division of the Ancien Régime, where everybody knows their place. All forms of behaviour, internal or external, national or international, only exist and are understood in terms of direct antagonism. This reached the point when some declared themselves as 'non-party supporters' and they did not need to state their reason or ask themselves what the abandonment of party lines meant".

Interpreting Medina Echavarría, we all knew the role that we were performing. Consequently, in that black and white world as he himself says, "to declare oneself a non-party supporter, meant that you were already taking a different position".

Stalin died in 1955 but it took a year for Stalinism to be criticised in the former Soviet Union. In the United States, McCarthyism was in retreat but its expansive wave had reached our shores a few years before.

Many of the States forming the present international community were still African and Asian colonies. The 1955 Bandung Conference inspired by Nasser, Nehru and Tito had just started to give voice to a third world anxious for autonomy.

Our Latin America started to think by itself above all through the ECLAC ideas. These ideas initiated years of fast growth, substituting imports, giving momentum to a modernisation that the great intellectual, Fernando Fajnsylber, referred to as unfinished modernisation because it did not close the gaps of exclusion, poverty, inequality and regional diversity. It did not strengthen, apart from a few examples, the solid democratic systems.

The Chile of 1955 was a country that had consolidated its continuing democracy. This made us all proud. We could breath the air of freedom and the respect for human rights. Our economy was advancing with difficulty - just 3 per cent annual growth - which was considered a success. I cannot resist advertising today's 6.2 per cent growth rate, indicated by the Economic Activity Monthly Monitor.

In addition to economic difficulties, we had persistent inflation. In 1970, we were ready to "celebrate" the uninterrupted record of Chile's inflation centenary: one hundred continuous years of inflation. And although, the State was begining to incorporate the middle and popular classes into the welfare system – there were many who were left out of the process, especially in the rural areas.

In those years, just over a third of our students were finishing secondary school – a third compared today's 95 per cent.

We were a country that looked at its development in an autarchic way, where the cordillera was enormous and the sea was infinite. This was a Chile which had World War II fresh in its memory and instead of drinking coffee we drank a milky water of fig coffee which we called coffee, and instead of drinking tea we used a kind of bark which produced a tint with a vague tea flavour.

In this country, in those years, imported goods were unusual, extravagant and something to which only a few had access, certainly not the students of this Faculty. It was another Chile with its pride but with tremendous limitations. It was a Chile, whose model of development was beginning to show the first signs of fatigue and where the redistributed State resources were decreasing despite the growing social demand.

A few years later, the phrase "Chile has to change" became a common phrase for all Chileans. We had different ideas of how we had to change but the fact that we had to change was not in question. It is difficult to express, in so many words, the magnitude of the change between that world and today's.

Since then, the country's foundations have been shaken. In a few decades, the world experienced changes that previously took centuries. The bipolar world that seemed destined to survive forever, fell down in months. The certainties of the world rapidly became uncertainties. Faith in irreversible progress opened the door to a sceptical vision of development where there was no established truth or direct road but rather questions and difficult, sinuous and steep roads to peace and welfare.

In those 50 years, Chile experienced an intense aspiration to change and enjoy greater justice. The desire to end the painful tragedy of our society, our democracy and human rights. From that abyss, we had to pick up the pieces of our history in order to accomplish today's success.

Building a country centred on the human being

The Chile, which is now returning to a democratic life, has had to reposition itself in a world that is radically different. Sometimes, whilst we fought to consolidate democracy in Chile we lost sense of the scale of change happening outside our borders, a world where autarchy had no place and where people were not constrained by time and space.

"In the present process of globalisation", as Manuel Castells says, "productivity, competitiveness, efficiency, communication and the power of society start from a technological capacity to process information and produce knowledge".

It is a state of affairs which allows emerging countries to skip development stages that was previously considered unthinkable in order to achieve better levels of development and welfare. But, at the same time, this process produces enormous inequalities if the necessary preventative measures are not adopted.

The world may be multipolar from the viewpoint of the existing major economic blocks. However, it is clear that today there is only one super power with the political and military resources to impose its ideas. For three hundred years, we have not experienced a situation like this. All international politics arose from the peace of the Westphalia Congress, in 1642, centred on the balance of European States, which later would become globally significant.

Foreign politics is conducted by finding a place within the global balance. Today, Chile conducts Foreign politics very well. During World War I, we were neutral; in World War II, we were neutral, until 1943, when we declared war against Germany and Italy. And Japan? I was once asked, "Ah, no, Chile played it safe. We declared war on Japan after Hiroshima and Nagasaki".

In today's world, we have had to integrate ourselves into international affairs and we are doing this actively and not passively, taking opportunities and defending ourselves from adversity without renouncing our identity but opening our doors to the world.

BASIS FOR DEVELOPMENT

We must compete tirelessly and to do this successfully we need a fairer and more cohesive country where everybody benefits from the fruits of growth. Chile has chosen both to perfect its democracy, to attain greater social justice, and also to grow in a sustainable manner.

These pillars allow us to aspire to reach the development threshold – a development that in our view is not measured by mere growth figures but, above all, by the levels of dignity achieved particularly by the underprivileged.

Our objective is to reach this level of development within a globalised world. To grow we need clear policies, particularly in the economic field, defined rules and to avoid populist temptations to shortcuts, which will surely lead us to the precipice. This is what we are doing, overcoming the false dilemma between the public and private sectors.

It is evident that today the market economy has an important role to play. It is the market, which generates economic dynamism, enterprise and investment, but the market on its own cannot respond to everyone's needs. In the market, people are valued for what they have; in Chile, all citizens are the same and have the same rights. That is why the State's responsibility to play a guiding and organising role in the public sector is irreplaceable.

Only the presence of what is public - the political will expressed by the people is what will ensure that growth will goes hand in hand with equity. And for this we need strong, clear and well-defined social policies.

DIFFERENCES WITH NEO-LIBERALISM

It is this point where there is a big difference with the neo-liberal world. Those in the neo-liberal world believe that the market by itself can reestablish the prerequisite conditions for a more equitable society. We know that economic growth alone is not enough. It is clear that society, through democratically defined public policies, must dictate which goods should be accessible to all citizens.

When we speak of "eight years of compulsory education" or

today "twelve", we are saying that the State must guarantee that all children have access to twelve years of schooling. The same applies to access to healthcare, the right to have a dignified home and to enjoy the benefits of social policies on housing, or to benefit from measures designed to eradicate poverty.

LATIN AMERICA

In brief, I think that a new concept has emerged in Latin America. A concept that has emerged not from theory but from a concrete reality of what has been happening.

The great challenge of our region is to create a social protection network to ensure cohesion while remaining competitive in the world. The countries that are affected by difficulties and social tension are often not competitive. Exactly the opposite of what happens in Europe; although it is true that perhaps due to their extensive social network, some believe that they are prevented from being competitive, given the costs involved.

Just because Europe is re evaluating their protection network doesn't mean we cannot have similar policies to those which the Europeans created some time ago. And this is, perhaps, the central question in this region.

Chile, because of its size (though with a small market), is dependent on integrating with global markets. And this is why we aim to associate ourselves with the strongest global economies, to the emerging economies and of course to the other economies of our region. This will allow us to contribute to clear, better and more equitable rules.

Nevertheless, this approach poses challenges of a more global nature. Globalisation has to be a process in which we both participate and observe and we must rise to this challenge. This is what we have attempted to do.

This brings us back to the importance of law, nationally and internationally. We have to create the necessary conditions to allow us to benefit from globalisation.

We cannot allow globalisation to be a wild and unmanageable

force. Globalisation cannot be allowed to become a tide that fatally pulls us towards a direction not of our choosing. It is imperative that with everyone's collaboration, especially that of the judicial system, we continue defending and adopting the type of supranational regulatory positions that allow us to achieve global peace, order and security.

LAW AND INTERNATIONAL COMMUNITY

If Nation States have been able to control matter through their national legal systems, thereby preventing the law of the jungle ruling their borders, would it be unreasonable to expect the same from the global community through investments of international law?

Perhaps posing this question might be considered Utopian, but it would also have been Utopian to believe in the contribution of the rule of law when we moved from feudal States to Nation States.

Also, let me say that, Utopias are only the dreams we are capable of having about a better world. And nothing and nobody should stop our capacity or indeed, our right, to conceive a better world, because a better world is not only necessary but also possible.

Who would have imagined that in little less than 50 years, since the 1948 Universal Human Rights Declaration in Paris, the theory and practice of fundamental rights would have achieved such international status? Would international agreements on civil and political rights have also qualified as Utopian? And then later, an international agreement on economic, social and cultural rights? The subsequent conventions on torture, racial discrimination and women? And, lastly, to envisage an International Penal Court charge with evaluating the most serious violations of human rights? That is the progress in 50 years. What do we propose to do in the next fifty?

Taking people's rights seriously is to take people themselves seriously. What is a person without the entitlement of their rights, without the possibility of being represented and having their rights enforced in national and international situations? The Executive, Legislature and Judiciary have enormous responsibilities in recognising and exercising these rights effectively, especially in what constitutes the fundamental rights of the human being.

A Faculty of Law also has a responsibility for research, education and promotion of human rights. That is why I was very pleased to learn that for two years this Faculty has operated the Human Rights Centre, which deals precisely with these matters.

The progress of Human Rights has been tremendous over the past century, with the expansion of fundamental rights, especially the recognition of economic, social and cultural rights – an expansion, which today includes the rights of individuals as well as the community. The multitude of peoples inhabiting the Earth are bearers of rights including the right to peace, to development and to a healthy environment at a global level. What are those rights if they are not collective rights?

With the emergence of the Kyoto Protocol recently, it is critical that the inadequate and irresponsible development strategies of the current generation are halted in order to avoid sacrificing the right of future generations to a healthy environment, free from contamination.

And this involves issues that are beyond our borders.

INTERNATIONALISM OF HUMAN RIGHTS

The process of the internationalisation of human rights, which started with the 1948 declaration, has certainly become more visible. The fundamental rights, approved internally within the States some centuries ago, are now incorporated into international law by virtue of agreements and treaties on the matter. It was just five decades ago, that a body of international law on human rights was formed with its treaties, agreements, courts of justice, etc.

Moreover, as these rights exist universally, they also exist regionally, and we speak of an inter-American human rights system, a European system, an African system of human rights, as well as a system for the Asia-Pacific region. And it is all part of the same process: how to achieve the dignity of the individual.

Nevertheless, I do not think that it is enough to proclaim rights -

we must make them effective. The world, including Latin America, has succeeded in enhancing personal rights and political rights, but there is still much to be done on economic rights. It is here where we have much to do, to achieve equality and solidarity.

And in this regard there is no better suggestion than that of Carlos Fuentes, the Mexican writer, when he says, "In our continent it is necessary that our political, economic, even moral imagination one day reaches our verbal imagination".

It is a fact that fundamental rights are related to individuals. In this sense, they are individual rights which apply to all human beings, which gives them a universality.

Solidarity, according to many, is a virtue not often discussed today. And this is why it is vital to have social policies which provide for the underprivileged.

A decent society is not only a society with individual liberties but also one, which applies itself to the elimination of progressive inequalities. What is the sense of having freedom of thought, expression, association and action, for people who live in extreme poverty? How can we face up to this reality?

Octavio Paz, another notable Mexican, recalling the French revolutionary cause was right in saying that "fraternity is greatly absent in our contemporary society" and that "it is necessary to do whatever is in our power to recover it as the bridge linking the values of freedom and equality".

FIFTY YEARS LATER

At the beginning, I said that there was a strong thread connecting these 50 years – it is the strong thread of our convictions. Today as yesterday, we want a Chile that is better and fairer.

Ever since the hard experiences of the dictatorship and the intolerance, and lessons learnt, we have restored our convictions and are now restoring the country. Fifty years on, I come to this Faculty not with the certainty of a paradigm or a vision of a 50's decade but with the firm and renewed support of the humanist foundation that has always guided our search.

Building a country centred on the human being

I am convinced that today's Chile is a better society in terms of rights and liberties than 50 years ago; it is also a more equal society. In inaugurating this academic year I applaud the fact that seven out of ten students in further education are first generation university entrants. Seven out of ten, whose parents never had the opportunities of a university. Is there still much to do? Of course.

Chile is today a more plural society, that is, more diverse and we perceive our diversity not as a threat but as a great benefit.

Chile is today a more tolerant society, composed of people and organisations of different beliefs, who live together in harmony and show an increasing acceptance of new and opposing ideas and appear ready to learn from this. Please excuse me for saying something out of context: the homage that different political sectors have paid to Gladys Marin save me from needing to comment further on how tolerant we have become as a nation.

We have experimented with a formidable and positive cultural change, which because it is right before us, has gone unnoticed. See for yourself, since you know this better than anybody - the reform of our penal system designed to protect people's rights better, has replaced the old legal system which was inadequate, inquisitive and secretive.

Notice how the country was able to engage in a keen debate on the death penalty, which was banned as a morally reprehensible response to certain offences.

Notice how we were able to free ourselves from an unacceptable level of cinema censorship, with nearly 1000 movies being abolished. I am not talking about pornographic movies; I am talking about works by Bergman, Scorsese, Bertolucci, Almodóvar and Woody Allen.

Notice how we have debated the importance of new legislation on family matters. Subjects as important as identity, marriage, divorce and justice for children. These are legislative results of which we can all feel proud, because they represent the normal code of an open society where nobody has the right to impose his/her own ideas.

Building a country centred on the human being

Notice the progress we have made on press legislation, allowing the media to carry out their daily work of scrutinising all levels of authority, whether economic, political, military or any other.

Notice the success of our policies on the prevention of unwanted pregnancies and the fight against sexually transmitted diseases, especially AIDS.

Notice also how today's young mothers-to-be cannot now be denied education or face suspension, nor be expelled from school.

THE HUMAN BEING AT THE CENTRE

The world we are building today, therefore, is a world which is focused on the human being, a world endowed with the freedom to think, create, reason and dream but also to discuss and make agreements.

A human being only enjoys the guarantee of freedom, with access to equal opportunities. That is the key to what we do, because we know that the human being is born free, but his opportunities diverge according to the cradle where he is born. Hence the absolute necessity of public policies which remove these inequalities thereby allowing the exercise of freedom.

And finally, I would like to invite this Faculty, to proclaim mankind's potential in today's Chile, and to encourage the new generation to carry the torch and to be strong in the conviction that in the years to come we will have greater freedom, more tolerance and better opportunities. In brief, to deepen our democracy with further democracy.

We will deliver to the next generation a sound country, which has an increasing vision of how to develop in the future. Very few times in our history have we had an idea of how to move forward. Each of the changes introduced by democracy and freedom have helped create this new Chile of which we talk.

These ideas will make sense if you think deeply about them and expand them and pursue the Utopia of a country and a world, where the human being is the axis, where we are all needed and nobody is expendable.

Building a country centred on the human being

THE IDEALS: FREEDOM AND EQUALITY

The ideals of 50 years ago are similar to those of yesterday and today. The way to develop and implement them is different because the world has changed, Chile has changed, knowledge has advanced, but the ideals of freedom and equality remain. Perhaps this idea could be summed up in the individual-community balance, the search to overcome terror and the anxiety of solitude.

In this new emerging world, there is perhaps too much individualism and we need to encourage more solidarity. There is too much individual ambition and little collective gain. We have to be capable of teaching that the great challenges of our cultural development, including social development and cohesion, are fundamentally collective responsibilities.

Fifty years ago collective responsibilities were essential. An individual's contribution was inconceivable outside the context of the community.

I would like to say that today these collective responsibilities are still important and are gaining strength in the social arena. Yes, socially, in non-governmental organisations, community groups, ethnic communities, student associations, parents committees, political parties, ecological movements, and gender organisations. A society blossoms when it is diverse, polychromatic, independent, and free.

A society should not promote the success of the individual over the community but must emphasise the re-invention of the community in tandem with the full development of the individual.

This is perhaps the greatest challenge we face at the start of the 21st Century - how we balance individual development with collective undertakings.

And this is perhaps the biggest challenge that your generation will have, those who are now starting out, with ideals that are similar to those of 50 years ago, but with the conviction, I believe, that you are nearer to achieving it.

Chile's latest step on the path to truth *

WHEN PEOPLE IN other countries think of Chile, they sometimes think of earthquakes. Indeed, from time to time, Chile is shaken by an earthquake. But there is also another kind of earthquake - that which affects a country's soul, the very essence of its being. And when that happens, we also feel the eyes of the world on us.

The days since Monday's publication of the report of the National Commission on Political Detention and Torture are just such a case. The report revealed for the first time to Chileans the truth about state responsibility for torture during the 1973-1990 military regime. It is a truth that they had previously only suspected, that some had denied, and about which others had remained silent. This truth is contained in the testimonies of more than 35,000 people, in Chile or abroad, out of which, after rigorous verification, 28,000 were accepted as valid. The remaining 7,000 will be reconsidered.

It would not, I think, be an exaggeration to describe this experience as unique in the world. The report is the work of a state commission that reached its conclusions over a period of a year, hearing and recording the personal testimony of each and every victim. In this way, Chile has been able - after three decades - to confront a dark chapter in its history, a deep abyss of suffering and torment.

Why did we undertake this difficult challenge? I would say it is because, ultimately, every society has to find the path along which truth meets history.

---

* *Article published in The Christian Science Monitor, Boston, United States of America, December 3rd 2004*

Chile's latest step on the path to truth

In 1988, the Chilean people were able, with joy and optimism, to defeat dictatorship by referendum. The entire world saw how Chile said "no," rejecting the plans of the authoritarian regime to maintain its hold on power. Just 15 years ago, in December 1989, we freely elected a president and a parliament, putting Chile back on the road to democracy.

Since then, we have advanced with maturity and prudence, but without pause, in demolishing the walls behind which truth was hidden.

The first step on this road was the Rettig Report, published in 1991, which attempted to give the clearest possible account of the worst violations of human rights - those that resulted in loss of life and disappearances - committed by agents of the state or private individuals for political ends. More than 3,200 names of the dead and disappeared were gathered, outlining what had occurred in Chile and what had never before been recognised.

Subsequently, we took measures to help those who had been forced into exile or who had lost their jobs for political reasons. Each step along this road was guided by three overriding principles: truth, justice and reparation.

In 1999, we established a Human Rights Roundtable where, for the first time, representatives of the armed forces, together with leading figures from human rights organisations and from different religious groups, agreed on what had happened in Chile. That was the first time that we spoke of the secret disposal of bodies and of prisoners thrown into the sea.

In 2003, this hard road posed an even more difficult challenge - that of setting up a commission where surviving Chileans, with their untold memories and pain, could be heard and, in this way, contribute with their testimonies to establishing truth in Chile and to healing the country's wounds.

I've been deeply moved by these thousands of testimonies - by the accounts of the victims. I've felt closely the magnitude of their suffering, the irrationality of the brutal cruelty they suffered, and the immensity of the pain. However, I believe that the courage to face this truth speaks well of Chileans and of the maturity we have attained. The report confronts us with an undeniable truth: Political detention and torture were institutional practices of the state. This was absolutely unacceptable and out of keeping with our nation's historic traditions.

Chile is, of course, not alone in having suffered such a chapter. It wasn't so long ago that Europe, which we now look to as a model of respect for human rights and individual liberty, went through a period in which the human rights of millions of its citizens were widely and terribly violated.

Yet history shows us that other countries suffering such experiences have healed the wounds of their past and built a present of freedom and prosperity - some with more ease than others. In none of them have memories been erased; instead, they have been transformed into part of a shared view of the past. And for new generations, the challenge is to preserve respect for human rights as part of a heritage shared by all of society.

In Chile, the work of this commission and the publication of its report has gone far beyond what many imagined. The testimony of each man and woman will be preserved in an individual file, forming part of the country's permanent archives.

Perhaps this is the most important step we can take to repair the victims' pain. We have put an end to their silence, restoring their dignity in the eyes of society. Of course, there will also be material reparation. It will be modest, but it symbolises the obligation of the State to recognise its responsibility, and the details will be debated by Congress.

But that is not what is most important. What is most important is that the light of truth now illuminates the coexistence of Chileans. Because we have been capable of looking, unblinkingly, at the hard truth, we can now begin to defeat the pain, to heal the wounds.

I have spoken to my country from the ethical dimension of political life. In this 21st century, that should be the anchor of relations within every society, and of the international community.

In Chile, we have understood that if we want never to repeat a dark chapter of our history, we must never again deny it.

Without democracy, there can be no progress *

WHEN THE COMMUNITY OF DEMOCRACIES was founded in Warsaw in 2000, Chileans participated actively, out of the conviction that democratic values are universal and part of our civilization's heritage. Universal democracy is not only possible, it's a necessity, and that is probably the great lesson of the 20th century.

Of course, as with any other constantly-evolving process, we should ask ourselves about the most relevant challenges of democracy. I think that as we enter the 21st century, there are four questions that come to mind and challenge us all.

First: How do we make democracy more than simply the act of participating in elections, and extend it so it becomes a system in which all citizens feel that their voices can be heard?

Second: How do we make sure that our economic growth also includes policies to ensure greater social cohesion, so that no one feels excluded from society?

Third: How can we adapt a common model of democratic practices to widespread cultural diversity?

Fourth: How can we express our identities as local communities in the light of the impact of globalisation?

Responding to these questions has been, perhaps, a constant theme over the past few years. What is our common project? Where do we want to go with this?

In the case of Chile, the first thing we learned over the past few years is that strengthening democracy in each and every one of

---

* *Excerpts from the speech to open the 3rd Ministerial Conference of the Community of Democracies, Santiago, Chile, April 28th 2005*

our institutions goes hand in hand with our ability to increase economic growth, justice and social equality, while also promoting the personal freedoms of the members of our society.

We have learned, then, that these reforms have to be simultaneous rather than successive. We have to take up all these tasks in their entirety, which is perhaps our greatest challenge.

Looking ahead, in order to increase development in our countries, we have to have more democracy, more growth, more freedom and more cultural diversity.

In Chile, we understand that the progress that we want to make is directly proportional to increases in the personal freedoms of our citizens, which lead to better opportunities and more rights for all. But democracy is at the root of progress and development. Without democracy, there can be no progress. There is no such thing as a dictatorship that brings progress to its people.

We have also learned that economic growth is a necessary condition to strengthen democracy, in order to improve the quality of life of the poorest among us. The legitimacy and credibility of democracy comes not only from institutions that work well, including the electoral process, but also from how well the economy is doing, and if it can encourage opportunities and generate more wealth. This is why some say that having a well-functioning market economy is enough, and the rest will come naturally.

This is a path that we have not followed. We've said that growth must go hand in hand with equality. Growth without distribution, and distribution without growth, lead inevitably to social and political crisis, and the loss of freedoms.

How much of what we are seeing in Latin American is related to the simplistic belief of a few people that distribution can only occur in the context of populism? In our experience this will end in failure, in the long run. And how many others think that growth is enough, and the rest will come naturally?

Our challenge is to enact social reforms for better employment, social welfare, education, housing and healthcare, with the same effort that we have made with economic and political reforms.

As the recently-deceased Italian philosopher Nolberto Bobbio

Without democracy, there can be no progress

wrote, "this is not just about strengthening the rule of democracy; it's also about building a demanding democracy." Such a democracy, he says, should be "able to temper the most obvious and unjust material inequalities. This is the way it must be, because the presence of these inequalities in any society make the use and enjoyment of democratic liberties an empty and illusory exercise for those who have less."

This is where we have to be able to combine the market, the fundamental engine of economic growth, with a democratic system in order to advance more quickly.

In this region of the world, Latin America, inequalities manifest themselves very obviously. The market is made up of consumers, who have unequal buying power. A country that only reflects the reality of the market ends up being a country rife with inequalities. Citizens, who are equal under the law, and in their rights and duties, build democracies. The market is essential for growth and democracy is essential for governance.

A free, productive system, with clear rules, is what brings the results of growth to everyone, as long as it respects the rule of law and has the lowest possible transaction costs. Meanwhile, we need a public policy to ensure that everyone receives the public services which meet their basic needs.

This is what we have learned over the years. But we have also evolved and you have seen that Chile is extraordinarily open to the world, maybe because we felt so far removed from the centres of global power for such a long period of our history. It's not easy to get here, it's a long flight, and we're also a small country, with just 15 million people. We have learned that the growth of our economy will always be tied to our ability to position ourselves on the world stage, in the largest markets.

We also want to interact with other cultures. Isolation in the 21st century is the antithesis of progress. This is why we are firmly in favour of multilateralism. If globalisation is to be the stage on which economics, finance, politics, trade and all the other activities of peoples and nations will be moving, we need to participate in universal forums, where we can meet, debate and set up agreements for the good of humanity. This is the very essence of multilateralism.

As globalisation spreads, new challenges arise. Debates about the environment lead to debates about the quality of life within our countries, but most environmental issues relate to decisions made beyond our borders. Where can we discuss these issues?

I think that differences may arise over many of these issues, but experience has increasingly shown that democratic countries can come to some kind of an understanding.

To illustrate our ability to understand one another, I would like to quote Thomas Jefferson, who said: "In every country where man is free to think and to speak, differences of opinion will arise from differences of perception and the imperfection of reason. But these differences, when permitted to purify themselves in free discussion, are but as passing clouds, spreading over our land transiently and leaving our horizon brighter and more serene."

This is exactly what this conference is about: there may be different perspectives in this debate among free men and women, but at the end, as Jefferson said, "when permitted to purify themselves in free discussion, they are but as passing clouds, spreading over our land transiently and leaving our horizon brighter and more serene."

Over the last few years, as others have said, the political landscape of the world, from Seoul to Santiago, has changed. There are many countries where we never thought we would ever see free elections but they eventually happened. It's a new playing field.

Every time we have an election and we achieve democracy, we also achieve the right to dream and to have more hope. The important thing is how to follow through with these dreams and hopes.

In a globalised world where international political issues often become local political issues. As others have said this evening, issues that seem far removed from democracy, like the Doha Development Round, end up influencing the development and the quality in life of our countries. What happens next December in Hong Kong, whether the Doha Round is successful, has to do, in the end, with the answer that I can give to a worker here in Chile

Without democracy, there can be no progress

about his ability to sell the goods he exports for a just price in a global world with fair trade rules.

This 3rd Ministerial Conference of the Community of Democracies is dealing with a political landscape that has changed since the meetings in Seoul and Warsaw. However, these challenges reflect humanity's infinite ability to move forward. Just as we ended slavery, today the key to the future lies in the recognition of equality of opportunity and rights among all human beings.

Chile 30 years later : The legacy of a crushed dream: 'Never again' *

THIRTY YEARS AGO, Chile had its own Sept. 11. Then too, an emblematic building fell victim to violence: the Moneda presidential palace, a symbol of the Chilean Republic that no one ever thought to see engulfed in flames, was destroyed. President Salvador Allende took his life there in a gesture that stirred the conscience of the world

Today, the Moneda palace is again the centre of Chile's government and the seat of its presidents. The white-walled palace is a focal point of Chile's civic life, and children, young people, families, and tourists wander through its courtyards. Chile is no longer a polarised country; today, it is a country in which consensus reigns, a country that is forging its way ahead amid the new challenges of a globalised world.

But every country is built on the foundations of its past. And, on this 30th anniversary of the military coup, Chileans are, as never before, seeking to untangle the truth of their past, to see what was once hidden, to hear spoken aloud what was only whispered, to read what could not be written. And visitors from around the world have come to see us and discover what our country is like 30 years after that coup.

"Never again" are the words on every Chilean's lips today. They

---

* *Article published in the International Herald Tribune, New York, United States of America, September 11th 2003*

Chile 30 years later: The legacy of a crushed dream: 'Never again'

are the fruit of deep reflection, of willingness to face the past with courage, in the awareness that it is history that will provide one, or more, interpretations of those events. This "never again" is anchored in a permanent commitment to democracy as the way to settle differences, and in a deep-rooted respect for human rights.

However, the 30th anniversary of that fateful day in Chile's history also raises another question: why did the coup, and its sequel of arrests, death, torture and exile, in such a remote country, have such a deep impact on the feelings and conscience of so many people around the world?

Perhaps it was because Allende represented the dreams of a generation when he attempted the unprecedented feat of advancing toward socialism through free elections and republican institutions. This was the time of the cold war, of a world divided, when words took on special meaning, and phrases, like social justice, anticolonialism or basic resources, immediately conjured up defining labels.

It was probably this utopian element that dazzled so many people around the world, especially in Europe. Allende captured it in his first message to Chile's Congress: "We are setting out on a new road; we are walking without a guide through uncharted territory."

The experiment ended in tragedy. No country can survive when dreams spill over, when polarisation exacerbates differences, and when the authority doesn't govern. Those were the mistakes. But, after Sept. 11, 1973, came the horror. That was when the solidarity of so many people in different continents provided us with refuge, and gave us time to heal our wounds and to think about the future. We will never be able to thank them enough.

Today, Chile is a different country. The first to lay aside their differences were the political parties that formed the Concertation for Democracy. We united and, 15 years ago, were able to say no to dictatorship, and to re-establish democracy. And today, the armed forces are fully integrated into that democracy. That is why we can now look at the events of 30 years ago through different eyes.

After our Sept. 11, the world began to be aware of human rights in a way never seen before. The other Sept. 11, in 2001, created a new awareness of terrorism as a threat to humanity. It is from these two great tragedies that we have emerged looking to the future in the conviction that intolerance and polarisation provide neither ethical nor political answers to the needs of people.

We do not want a world split into those who benefit from globalisation and those who do not, into those who are within the system and those who are outside it. That is why we believe it is so important to draw up new norms and rules that fit the realities of today's world. Chile is ready to cooperate in this international effort. More than half of the Chileans alive today had not been born in 1973, but we all know that in order to advance toward the future, we must start from the lessons of yesterday.

Chapter 2

Europe, Latin America and the Caribbean:
To renew the long standing relations

The EU, Latin America and the Caribbean: Ten areas for collaboration *

SPAIN'S RECENT PRESIDENCY of the European Union was a period of particular significance for Chile. The achievements of those six months, of course, included the signing of Chile's Association Agreement with the European Union's fifteen Member States. For us, that is a great source of satisfaction.

But they also included the Second EU-Latin American and Caribbean Summit, an event that we should evaluate not only in the light of current events, but also in its implications for the longer-term tendencies and enduring characteristics of our bilateral ties. In times of turbulence, it is especially important that we have clear long-term goals and that we do not deviate from our common path. And, precisely, during Spain's presidency of the EU, we have seen the emergence of such strategic guidelines.

In May 2002, when the heads of state and government of our two regions met in Madrid, it was their second Summit. However, it was the first to take place in this twenty-first century and it was also the first since the terrorist attack on the Twin Towers, with all its implications in terms of rethinking global security.

Without doubt, it was more than just three years which separated the First Summit, held in Rio de Janeiro in 1999, and the Madrid Summit. In the intervening period, the world became aware, in many different ways, of the reality of globalisation. And

---

* *Article published in El País, Madrid, Spain, July 9th 2002*

The EU, Latin America and the Caribbean

it also became aware that globalisation must be given direction and a human face if inequality is not to undo what we have achieved through democracy.

We will have missed the key point if we see globalisation only in terms of market forces or of the power of nations. What is happening in the world today goes far beyond that. With globalisation, new problems have emerged to which we must jointly seek urgent answers. There has never been any automatic way of reducing inequality and that is also true today for the inequality, instability and crises brought by globalisation.

The globalisation we seek requires rules and institutions that are capable of regulating it commercially, financially, technologically, judicially, environmentally, socially and culturally. If we want to achieve such rules and institutions, we have a duty to maintain confidence in the ability of today's emerging global politics to provide society with the necessary leadership.

The agenda for this common objective can be defined in many different ways. But, as I said in Madrid, I believe it is possible to identify ten areas in which we have taken a similar position in the past and in which we can continue to work together. I am convinced that working together makes a difference.

In my view, political cooperation between the European Union, on the one hand, and Latin America and the Caribbean, on the other, is possible in the following areas:

Disarmament policies;

The struggle against terrorism;

United Nations' peace missions;

Policies that seek to liberalise international trade and put an end to protectionism;

Support for the International Criminal Court;

The defence of human rights and democracy;

The fight against racism, xenophobia and other forms of discrimination;

The protection of the environment;

The combat of drug trafficking and cross-border organised crime;

Scientific and technological development.

These are areas in which we have the capacity to coordinate our activities and to increase international cooperation. We have seen this in the launch of bilateral talks between our two regions in the United Nations, in its different specialised organisations and in international bodies related to world economic development.

Of course, in many ways, Europeans and Latin Americans are different, but we are bound by our vision of the future as well as by our roots, by the centuries of culture through which we can trace the origins of our identity. And the wealth of that history is an essential component of our dialogue today. In addition to the similarity between our shared values, there is an affinity between our political systems, in what we seek as societies and in our foreign policies.

Our countries have taken a similar position on the important issue of climate change. Our two regions have promoted democracy and respect for human rights with the greatest vigour.

It is my belief that in Latin America, we aspire to, and require, the social cohesion that Europe has achieved. It is in these very well-defined areas that our positions have gradually drawn closer and in which we can develop new initiatives that will allow us to address the challenges of the twenty-first century with confidence.

This is the great opportunity left for us by the period in which Spain presided over the European Union. Great changes will not happen overnight. They will require perseverance, political imagination and new ways of achieving governance, participation and equity for the citizens of our two continents. But if the goals of our work are clear, the results will create ever greater confidence and trust. And it is this confidence and trust that will allow our two regions to find common answers to the great challenges of our age.

2003 Canning Lecture: How this world is being organised? *

When, in 1826 the former British Foreign Minister George Canning said before the House of Commons: "I have called the new world into existence to redress the balance of the Old World", he was referring to the start of relations with some newly born Latin American countries. And as Canning viewed the world, almost two centuries ago, it seems to me that once again we are witnessing the birth of a new world. Two hundred years ago he was speaking of a new geographic world, that of Latin America.

A new world

Today we are witnessing a new world of a different kind. And major changes in the way the world is organised. The question is how should we approach this new world, which is emerging before our eyes, at the beginning of the 21st Century?

First, we face the integration of a global society, a process people call globalisation, which is eroding both traditional ways of living and the formulation of public policies. Globalisation is about more than just increasing trade or global integration or the way we do business. Since it is much more than that this, it is

---

* *Transcript of the lecture delivered on July 14th 2003 in Lancaster House, London, United Kingdom*

expected that a new kind of society will emerge.

Secondly, on many fronts of this new world, conventional wisdom has become either too narrow or too broad. In my days as a graduate student you learnt that Mr Keynes used to say that you could give up many things except the sovereignty of the Bank of England when dealing with interest rates. With due respect to the Bank of England, we do not know what might happen if the United Kingdom decides to join the Euro tomorrow. Who is then going to decide on interest rates? At least in our case, even though we are a small country, our businessmen look to Chile's Central Bank for interest rate decisions as well as the country's risks and our adherence to financial policies.

Thirdly, I do not think the world is split into two political and military blocks anymore. There is just one big political superpower and this is a new scenario.

More recently, three additional factors have come into play. First, the larger countries that were the drivers of the global economy are slowing down. It is the first time for many years that Japan is not the economic power it once was. Europe has been unable to become the engine of growth that we hoped would resist the decline of the American economy. We therefore have these three major blocks or economic growth areas that are not performing very well. Second, the horror of September 11th, followed by other terrorist attacks, is presenting a tremendous new challenge. And thirdly, we have the crisis of the UN Security Council in dealing with Iraq that I believe represents a departure from the way we used to deal with these kinds of international problems.

Therefore this represents the current situation and there is clearly no single way to view our world. This morning, at the Progressive Governance Summit, Chancellor Gerhard Schroeder was talking about the challenges of demography and how Germany should address its ageing population and the growing demand for social security benefits. And to put it bluntly, he said that it is impossible to keep social pensions at their current levels if Germany wants to remain competitive. In other words he is saying that something needs to be done and this German experience is replicated all over the world. It is a world growing richer in diversity, culture and personal beliefs. We have greater diversity than in the past. At the same time, we have learnt that the way we manage our public policies will also be different because of these global issues. We believe there are many challenges to be met and the goals and beliefs of Latin American countries are similar to those of Europe.

THE IMPERATIVES TO ACHIEVE AN AGENDA FOR THE FUTURE.

We have learnt the hard way that in addition to democracy and respect for human rights we need responsible macroeconomic policies, with a balanced fiscal budget in order to keep our economy growing. In Chile, the GNP doubled in the 90s and we were able to reduce poverty levels from 40 per cent to 20 per cent of the population. At the same time, we know that we need to strengthen our democratic system and improve our democratic institutions. We have to learn how to heal the wounds of past human right violations. We are working on it because we want to debate an agenda for the future and not an agenda the past. If diversity is a hallmark for the future and if change is the hallmark of our civilisation, the dilemma is; what kind of policy should we pursue in order to have a better world? In Chile we are trying to fulfil all the requirements of the Washington Consensus as well as pursuing public and social policies to ensure that our growth rate allows us to reduce poverty and have improved healthcare, education, social housing, etc. And I think that even though we are portrayed as very good students with regard to our economic policies, I would say that while these economic policies are a necessary condition for success they are not sufficient for countries in Latin America.

PUBLIC – PRIVATE PARTNERSHIP

Allow me to give you just one example: We have today in Chile half a million students in higher education. This represents a tremendous increase from the two hundred thousand we used to have ten years ago. Of these half a million, only 20 per cent have parents who went to university, and the remaining 80 per cent are the first generation of their families to attend higher education, representing a tremendous change in terms of social mobility and therefore extremely important. How does one finance those students in higher education? During my time I went to a public university. But is it now possible to have free university for all? After discussing this with Prime Minister Tony Blair the idea arose of a student loan system to cover tuition fees which is to be repaid to the State, and this indicates the type of new thinking required when addressing social policies. I believe the way we used to run public policies, particularly in the social area, has changed significantly. Our GNP revenue sources have changed. Today the private sector is the driving force, representing more than 80 per cent of our economy. At the same time it is necessary to reform the way we run the government and this is what we have been trying to accomplish. This implies that in addition to the right economic policies the necessary social policies must be developed. The social policies that were defined and implemented by the State or the government in the past are now often carried out by the private sector.

Another example illustrates the point. Chile did not used to have any kind of unemployed benefit. We introduced unemployment insurance to be applied to the private sector employer and employee. This fund is run by the private sector through a bidding process. In other words, the money comes from workers and businessmen and will be run by an institution or company in the private sector that offers the minimum cost of administration. We aim to have more than one in five workers in the fund, accounting for over one million beneficiaries and which will represent 1.5 per cent of our GNP savings, once the fund is established.

In 1920, Chile had 4 years of compulsory education. In the 60's, it rose to 8 years and now we have extended it to 12 years. That is a decision taken by the citizens. In other words, the decision about how many years of schooling is required is now a public matter but the private sector can also help to tackle this issue. And this is what we are doing. When I was the Minister for Public Works we realised that the cost of developing a national system of highways would take up the whole budget, leaving nothing for the secondary roads to rural, poor and isolated areas. So we decided to introduce the BOT System and to open up the national highways to the private sector. Today, five billion US dollars – a very substantial amount of money by Chilean standards – has been invested by the private sector in our national highway system and we are spending more money than ever before.

Public money is directed to those areas where the private sector would never go. So using the private sector to fund public policies is one way of growing and being able to finance what the public needs. We have a tremendous problem in our judicial system, particularly for those who are in prison. By the end of my term we aim to double the number of square metres built for those in prison and we are going to double the number of prisons. All of these will be built with private money, the private sector will provide the beds and the food. The State will provide the police to care for those who are in prison. This is a new way to fulfil the decisions taken at governmental or parliamentary level by citizens that cannot be implemented in any other way.

INTEGRATION WITH THE WORLD

It is in this area where we in Chile have been able to provide some grounds of common understanding with regard to our public policies. The country, as a whole, has understood that it's development and growth will be determined principally through integration into the world. As you know, we are a small country of 15 million people and have decided that if this is a global world we have to be part of the global world. And that is why we took the unilateral decision to reduce our tariffs as well as negotiate free trade agreements with a number of other regions. This decision was based on a general view of how Chile is going to develop in this century and I do understand that other countries in our region have different views. If we talk about large countries such as Brazil and Argentina, I recognise that their domestic markets are extremely important to them.

Sixty-five per cent of Chile's GNP is represented by exports and imports; therefore, it is essential to see how we fare and how we are going to integrate into the world. We used to have a flat tariff of 11 per cent and in 1997 Chile decided unilaterally to reduce tariffs by 1 per cent within 5 years. Today we have a 6 per cent flat tariff across the board - and even lower given our Free Trade Agreements with Europe, the United States, Canada, Mexico, most Latin American countries, South Korea, and the European Free Trade Association (EFTA). This means that next year our tariff will be, on average, less than 3 per cent. Yes, less than 3 per cent. It is true; it is not an easy task. We used to have about 200,000 textile workers which has reduced to 30,000. But today we are exporting textiles to Europe and the USA and we are competing with other Asian nations who specialise in this sector. This is how the world acts today and therefore integrating our country into the world is a strategic decision of the Chilean people.

In our Free Trade Agreement negotiations with Europe and the US we always have private sector and labour representatives accompanying our negotiators. President Bush could not believe it when I told him that members of our labour unions would be present in Washington for the treaty negotiations. This dynamic approach is understood by all Chilean stakeholders that share the view that it is an opportunity for our country to diversify its exports, to search for new markets and to create new opportunities abroad. This is why we believe we are now in a better position to strengthen the integration process with the rest of the world. To compete and succeed in world markets a country needs to have social cohesion and, in this respect, public policies are essential.

In Europe you have a tremendous welfare state and a crucial decision still to be made is what you are going to do in this area if you want to remain competitive and at the same time maintain the necessary social cohesion. Our case is perhaps the opposite. We need to decide what kind of social network (I do not like the expression welfare state) that we need in order to achieve social cohesion in our society so that all of us have a sense of sharing in the growth of our economy. We have in place unemployment insurance and a pension fund that is being developed, and an educational system that is fair. In order to have similar opportunities we have to discriminate and we have to provide even more to those who have less. This is essential and very obvious if we are to share the benefits of growth to all, and be part of the international community. This is why it is so important that as Chile integrates into the world every citizen believes that the benefits of integration will reach every corner of Chile and all its communities, not just the capital and those areas already integrated into the global economy. And I understand it is my duty as President to aim for this. This is essential and is why I think that our international policy is so important, since to some extent we are linked to what happens in the rest of the world.

In today's conference (the Progressive Governance Summit), we were all listening to Mr Schroeder and asking ourselves how the German economy will again become the engine of Europe and eventually the engine of the world. Everybody hopes that the reforms being introduced in Germany will be successful. Because in the world what happens here, today, will affect us tomorrow. Chile belongs to Latin America and therefore practices its foreign policy from a regional perspective even though it also participates in the benefits of the global economy.

CHILE IS PART OF LATIN AMERICA

Allow me to be very clear with you on this issue. It is one thing to have strategic alliances to maximize our trade performance but at the same time it is essential to understand that, in order to compete in the world, some rules need to be in place if we are to create a better place for everybody. Chile is part of Latin America. We share its geography, history and culture and we are confident that it is possible for us to work together within our own region. This is why we think Mercosur is so important as a political arena of understanding and given what Europe has accomplished in terms of integration, we believe that it is possible to do the same in our region. Nevertheless, in order to have economic integration in the region it is essential to have some kind of physical integration with regard to infrastructure. You did that in Europe, and this is a tremendous challenge that still faces us in Latin America.

At the same time the fact that Mercosur is a customs union has made it very difficult for our low tariff rate to be integrated into Mercosur's much higher level of customs duties. Therefore, it does not make sense to be part of Mercosur's high tariff environment. That is why Chile is just an associate member of Mercosur. Nevertheless, we have many common issues with other Mercosur countries especially in ways to tackle agricultural subsidies. This morning everybody was happy about the new Common Agricultural Policy agreed by the European Union. This is important for the forthcoming WTO Cancun conference in September 2003. I also think that it is going to be very important for Chile, as an associate member of Mercosur, to push for progress in other areas.

Frankly speaking we can have similar tariffs but if a country devalues by 20, 50 or 100 per cent then it will affect the outcome of national macroeconomic policies. Therefore if one is going to promote integration among Latin American countries it will be essential to have something like the Maastricht Treaty. A realistic and binding general agreement. Otherwise it is impossible. It is not realistic and will not work to say: a 10 per cent flat is going to be your tariff and each party has different economic policies. This is why Chile has been trying to push in the other direction in the conviction that, in the end, it is the only approach that will produce serious results for everybody.

We are confident that after what has happened in the region, including the elections in Brazil and Argentina, we will be able to pursue some serious avenues of integration among Mercosur countries. But it is also important for us to work at a more international or global level. The combination of our network of global Bilateral Free Trade Agreements combined with a regional approach to trade, financing, public policies, etc, vis-à-vis the rest of the world is important to us. Let me be clear on this: if we are going to participate in the global world, rules will have to be established at that level. I know the issue is very difficult but unless we have some global rules, it will be difficult to compete. What happened yesterday, with the US imposing tariffs was not the right step to take. I understand that there may be some kind of dumping, but then lets discuss anti-dumping legislation. It is a difficult issue. However, on European agricultural policy we are probably closer to America. In the area of anti-dumping, we are closer to Europe and Japan, and in Doha we had a common front with Japan and Europe vis-à-vis the US.

This is the world in which we are living. If you are able to make progress on agricultural policy, the US will probably advance in the area of intellectual property rights. This is something that will be discussed in Cancun, Mexico. We have to think what future organisations and institutions are required and what rules are needed to ensure fair competition. The existence of rules that result in fair interaction is vital. It is a difficult but possible task. Our optimism derives from the fact that a small country like Chile has decided to have its own, broad network of Free Trade Agreements as our considered approach to global integration. It is extremely important to look at what can be done in that area and how to harmonise different approaches.

The issue of financing development illustrates the point. Many countries still speak in terms of developed or under-developed and I think this is no longer correct. We can talk about development aid when referring to Africa, but I do not think it has any meaning to discuss development aid when one is talking about many Latin American countries. Given their per capita income they do not qualify any longer for aid, and it is much more relevant for them to have access to international financial markets.

We want trade not aid. But then the question is: What are the rules of trade? Today, arranging financial agreements with a country in a high risk category is much cheaper to go to Wall Street than with the World Bank. It was not so 20, 30 or 40 years ago. It is a fact that countries that do not normally need money from abroad are the ones that can obtain the best interest rates. When I ask my Minister of Finance why we do not go to the World Bank he replies to me "Oh no Mr President, you are quite wrong, we have to issue bonds in Wall Street". Chilean bonds are doing well on Wall Street and are much cheaper than the World Bank. This is the new world and it is quite different from what we experienced 40 years ago. These are the new issues we have to discuss at a global level. To some extent this situation is a result of a number of your institutions that were created following the Second World War. This is going to be an extremely difficult issue to tackle but we will do it. What was the World Bank? The World Bank was the International Bank for Reconstruction which had the task of reconstructing Europe. And somebody at the last minute added the word "development" and the official title came into being: International Bank for Reconstruction and Development. However, reconstruction was the idea behind the bank and that happened in 1944. How many things have changed since then? The IMF was primarily concerned with fixing the exchange rate between developed countries, and Mr Keynes and Mr White discussed it. Needless to say, Mr White represented the US and therefore his plan was finally adopted.

When and where we will tackle these issues is open to question. The same applies to both the political multilateral institutions that emerged after World War II and the discussion over the future of the Security Council.

With regard to the Security Council, I will only say that in relation to Iraq it is probably true to say that it is easier to win a war than to win the peace after the war. This is a particular area where the work of the Security Council is going to be essential, particulary in the re-building of a post war Iraq. And despite the fact that we worked very hard with Prime Minister Blair to find a solution in the middle of the crisis, I think all of us failed in the Security Council. It is in this area where we believe our relationship with Europe is extremely important, not only in terms of trade with our most important partners – 34 percent of Chile's trade is with Europe – but also in terms of the common values we all share, the respect for human rights, democracy, the understanding of the market's role and the value of social cohesion in all our societies.

After the 20th Century we recognised that diversity is part of the richness of spirit in a particular society. Therefore, when we reached the Free Trade Agreement with Europe, we did much more than that: we signed an agreement of co-operation and of political identity. The Association Agreements signed by Chile and Mexico with the EU are the first steps to future agreements. They will open new areas of cooperation in the fields of technology, biotechnology, and science. We do some things the right way and we are still learning in others. We have a lot to learn from what you have done in building bridges between the universities and business communities. It will be essential to build bridges of freedom, democracy, human rights, the rule of law, free and fair trade, culture – all of these have the same meaning on both sides of the Atlantic and this is why we think this new emerging world will enjoy the stability afforded by these rules.

You have the Treaty of Nice, the European Constitution and you are the masters of how to build this process of integration. We would like to learn from you and share what you have been able to achieve with the rest of the global world. This is essential to us and given that Chile and Latin America have such special relations with Europe, we see the United Kingdom as an important partner. Today we have a new framework with the UK – a powerful tool to strengthen these relations that is represented by the Association Agreement between Chile and Europe. We also have a common heritage. The names of O'Higgins, Lord Cochrane, O'Brien and Mackenna are but a few in the history of our country. We did not know what to do with our freedom, having just gained our Independence from Spain. It was in those years that many people from this island travelled to Chile to help us take our first steps as an independent nation. Today, the British spirit is present in the development of many sectors such as mining, defence, water supplies, banking, trade, etc. As well as the political and cultural areas and this is why we think that strengthening our relations and bilateral links between our two countries is so important because it will reinforce and diversify the dynamism of our ties. Last Saturday in London, we signed an agreement on double taxation and I hope that this represents an important step forward in the inter-change between both countries.

This morning the Chilean Finance Minister and some representatives of our business community met with more than 100 British businessmen to discuss common investment and interests. It is here where we think we have much to do. I am also attending this evening a working dinner hosted by the Lord Mayor with members of the business community. Prime Minister Tony Blair and I have agreed to strengthen our political relations and our common effort to boost relations with Europe and Latin America and the Caribbean. If we can continue along this path, I truly believe we have much to learn from each other.

Let me conclude with a reflection by Bernardo O'Higgins – Chile's national hero and the son of an Irish man - who studied in England and said that if Chile maintained good relations with Britain it could establish success on basic principles. We shall establish our success on mutual relations. This is it; we shall establish our mutual success on basic principles – the principles that lie behind common policies and a decision to build a new partnership in this new emerging world. The problem is that the tools of the past almost certainly have to be changed given the new realities and that in order to maintain our success it is essential that these basic principles should prevail. Basic principles by which we are able to discuss the kind of trade we envisage, the rules which will apply, and how we will apply them are all on the agenda. This lies behind Chile's strategic decision to be part of the world and to compete because we know that we can do so successfully.

Thank you very much to Canning House for the opportunity to share some of these ideas with you this evening.

The European-Southern Hemisphere relationship *

EUROPE IS, in a sense, also our home. From Europe we have learned a lot, and there is much still to learn. From the Greeks we learned how to grasp the ethos of an era. From the Christians we learned the absolute value of the human being. From the peoples of Europe we have learned that freedom is the basis of our political action.

And more recently, Europe has taught us that this twenty-first century needs strong and efficient regional entities. We have learned that this is a time of political concentration. When we, Latin Americans, look at today's Europe we see an example to follow. We have to work for a more united and integrated Latin America. It is the only way we can have a voice in this globalised world.

It is a time of concentration. We need political cooperation to overcome the asymmetries of the present globalisation. Europe and the south share the main challenge of how to make globalisation work for the many and not only for the few. It means trade, development aid, but also political and cultural agreements. And for this challenge, the Progressive Governance Network is the main forum where progressives from all continents can collaborate and cooperate politically in order to ensure these goals come true.

We, progressives from Europe and from the South, are at times both alike and different. Different because we proceed from diverse histories, geographic locations and distinct levels of development that highlight different priorities and problems; and alike because

* *Edited version of the speech delivered in the Progressive Governance Conference, Budapest, Hungary, October 14th 2004*

we share the common democratic values of respect for human rights, social equity and freedom, values which we consider are universal and which we believe should determine the future.

We share common thinking. We see the changes in progress more as an opportunity than as a danger and the challenges of the future attract us more than the nostalgia for the past. This is the reason why we identify ourselves as progressives.

ABOUT GLOBALISATION

Consequently it is with that vision that we approach the vertiginous process of change and transformation, which is characterised by the globalisation of financial markets, increasing international trade, the globalisation of scientific and technological activities, as well as the fact that productivity and competitiveness depend more and more on the capacity to generate knowledge and the efficient processing of information.

To be positive about these unavoidable changes resulting from globalisation does not mean one has to have unilateral views. At the same time we see the great opportunities that this process opens up for humanity, in all fields. We are also aware of the complex effects that it could bring to the social, political and cultural lives of millions of human beings.

The globalisation process generates an increasing and unbalanced interdependence, with brutal changes in productivity, acute competition, and increasing inequality within societies and among nations.

We see a loss of social cohesion, persistently high levels of unemployment, widening wage gaps, and greater concentration of wealth. Many traditional mechanisms of social integration have lost their efficacy and their capacity to break the intergenerational transmission of inequity. New types of horizontal exclusion are created, social disintegration occurs where not only the poor are excluded but the rich abandon the public space. All these phenomena produce a decline in the quality of living.

The great challenge for all of us is to manage the positive

aspects of these changes and avoid the negative effects. How can we achieve real modernisation that allows the fruits of progress to enter the homes of all citizens and all the worlds nations?

The United Nations Millennium Declaration "to ensure that globalisation becomes a positive force for all the world's people" has now become standard. This has been the strong view of international civil society since Seattle. However, all these positive processes have led to very limited action.

The trend towards the amplification of international inequalities in recent decades can be attributed not only to renewed international disparities in per capita GDP levels, but also to widespread inequalities within countries. In fact, during the period 1975 to 1995, 57 per cent of the population in a sample of 77 nations were living in countries in which income distribution was worsening. Only 16 per cent lived in nations in which it was improving. The remainder lived in countries with stable levels of inequality or ones in which no clear trend could be identified.

Social equity is the moral imperative of our times. In this globalised world, poverty and injustice cannot be hidden anymore. We cannot seek to reduce uncertainty for business while leaving the poor unprotected from the most basic contingencies of life: sickness, unemployment, old age and death. We cannot reform judicial systems to protect property rights without recognising the lack of protection of the basic rights of the citizen. We cannot celebrate the economic and technical progress of this century and turn a blind eye to the millions who cannot satisfy their elementary needs.

Consequently, in the same way that developed countries have reworked the classic Welfare State model to face the competitive challenge presented by globalisation and the new economy, developing countries face the task of overcoming unbearable social inequities to ensure competitiveness. This will involve investment in human capital and in social safety nets, to extend their coverage to ensure more efficient, transparent and effective social expenditure, more efficient and comprehensive systems, and specific mechanisms to create solidarity and equity.

Social inequity both exacerbates social and political conflict and stimulates populist movements and economic experiments. Social inequity thus increases the volatility of policies and impedes macroeconomic stability.

We need to move social equity into the mainstream of public policy and to turn it into a solid foundation for long-term growth. We have to think strategically, identifying key areas for action and build solid alliances with civil society, private business, and foreign investors.

THE OBJECTIVES

The deficiencies shown by the current globalisation process have demonstrated, as has been stated by ECLAC, the need to work towards three key objectives:

First, guaranteeing an adequate supply of global public goods; Second, building a human rights-based world system, i.e., global citizenship; Third, gradually overcoming the asymmetries that characterise the world's economic system.

I am sure that we, Europe and the South, can work together for these goals. The worldwide support that the Fund Against Hunger and Poverty has achieved, is a strong signal that political concentration can work in this globalised world.

The first of these objectives focuses on the management of interdependence between nations. The other two focus on equity, in its two dimensions: between citizens and between nations. After some remarks on the first two objectives, I will deal at greater length with the third, which plays an essential role in guaranteeing equitable economic development at the global level.

In a broad sense the concept of global public goods includes, among others: international peace and justice, human knowledge, cultural diversity, the fight against international pandemics, environmental sustainability, the regulation of the use of global rules that regulate international economic transactions, and world macroeconomic and financial stability. What should be emphasised is the huge gap between the recognition of the growing importance of interdependence, and thus, of global public goods, and the weakness of the existing international structures - decision-making, financing and management - that guarantee their existence.

On the other hand, building global citizenship in a heterogeneous international community implies both respect for basic human rights, as well as cultural diversity, thus reconciling the principle of equality with the 'right to be different'. In this view, civil and political rights form an indivisible, interdependent whole, with economic, social and cultural rights.

The third objective implies that, just as redistributive action by the state is essential at the national level to ensure equality of opportunity, national efforts can succeed at the global level only if they are complemented by international cooperation designed to overcome the basic asymmetries of the global order, which are at the root of the profound international inequalities in income distribution.

THE ASYMMETRIES

These asymmetries fall into three basic categories. The first is associated with developing countries' greater macroeconomic vulnerability to external shocks, which also constrain their limited means of coping with them. The net effect of this situation is that whereas industrialised countries have greater room for manoeuvre to adopt counter-cyclical policies and encourage stability of financial markets, developing economies have almost no such room at all. This is because financial markets tend to accentuate cyclical variations and market forces expect national authorities to behave pro-cyclically.

The second type of asymmetry is the concentration of technological progress in developed countries. The spread of technical progress from the originating countries to the rest of the world has continued to be 'slow and irregular'. This reflects prohibitive entry costs into technological activities and the constraints faced by developing countries from entering mature sectors. In these cases opportunities for developing countries are largely restricted to the attraction of multinationals that are already established in those sectors. In turn, the transfer of technology is subject to the payment of innovation rents, which are being given increasing protection by the international spread of intellectual property rights.

A third asymmetry is associated with the contrast between the high degree of capital mobility and the limited international mobility of labour, especially among low-skilled workers. This element is important, as asymmetries in the mobility of production have a regressive impact, since they work to the benefit of the more mobile factors of production, capital and skilled labour - and to the detriment of the less mobile factors, such as unskilled labour.

WHAT CAN WE DO?

I am convinced that to achieve success it requires the effort of every country. It is through our efforts that, despite being a small somewhat remote country, we have earned a modest place in the globalised world. We have achieved this not because of wealth, geopolitics or power, but on the basis of innovative ideas and the rich experience of our reform programme.

Correcting the first of these asymmetries implies that a comprehensive approach should be adopted to reduce the segmentation and volatility of developing countries' access to international financial markets. They also need to adopt counter-cyclical macroeconomic policies.

Correcting the second implies that the trading system should allow the smooth transfer of raw material production, technological mature industries and standardised services to developing countries. It also necessary to accelerate the developing countries' access to technology and guarantee their increased participation in the generation of technology in the higher-technology branches of production. To facilitate these processes, the trading system should give adequate room for the adoption of active domestic production strategies in developing countries.

Finally, overcoming the third asymmetry implies that labour migration should be included on the international agenda, both through a global agreement on migration policy as well as regional and subregional agreements.It also requires the adoption of complementary mechanisms that allow migration (such as the universal recognition of educational achievements and the transferability of pension and other social security benefits).

In the absence of suitable institutions to guarantee these three objectives, globalisation is proving to be a highly degenerative force, both at the international and the national level, as well as a factor in the erosion of social cohesion. This places an enormous demand on governance, at all levels. Without a suitable international framework, the insufficient supply of global public goods and the inequality-generating forces spawned by international asymmetries, national development will be hindered.

This implies that efforts at building strong institutions for a better global order should be based on a network of world, regional and national institutions, rather than being limited to one, or a few, international institutions.

Managing counter-cyclical macroeconomic policies is not an easy task, as financial markets generate strong incentives for developing countries to overspend during periods of financial boom and to over-adjust during crises. Moreover, globalisation places limits on national autonomy and exacts a high cost in terms of credibility when national policy instruments are poorly administered.

In an open environment, such as that which characterises the southern economies today, there should be systemic competitiveness based on three fundamental pillars: the creation of innovation systems to speed up the accumulation of technological capacities; support for new productive activities and the formation of production linkages; and the provision of quality infrastructure services.

Because of the key role of knowledge, any such strategy must be based on increased public and private investment in education, vocational and business training, and science and technology. The strategy should focus on creating dynamic innovation systems. In view of the intrinsic importance and crosscutting nature of new information and communication technologies, efforts to promote their active use are of vital importance in contemporary innovation systems.

The concept of 'public policy' should be understood in a broad sense, as any organised form of action aimed at achieving objectives of collective interest, rather than as a synonym for government actions. This definition of 'public' is in keeping with an awareness of the need to open up opportunities for civil society. It is also consistent with the need to overcome a crisis of the State that characterises many countries, and to correct both 'market failures' as much as 'government failures'. This approach emphasises the importance of attaining a high 'institutional density', in which a wide range of social actors participate actively, and are accountable to the citizenry, we call this high 'democratic density'.

Institution building, in this sense, recognises that development comprises broad goals, an idea that is implicit in the concepts of sustainable human development or the more recent concept of 'development as freedom'. These concepts are obviously expressions of long-standing and deeply rooted elements of development thinking. This is the only way to confront the strong centrifugal forces that characterise private affairs today. Indeed, in many parts of the developing (and industrialised) world, people are losing their sense of belonging to society, their identification with collective goals and their awareness of the need to develop ties of solidarity. It means, in other words, that all sectors of society need to participate more actively in democratic political institutions and that a wide range of mechanisms should be developed within civil society itself to strengthen relationships of social solidarity and responsibility and, above all, to consolidate a culture based on a sense of a collective identity and a tolerance for diversity.

For this we have to overcome the incompleteness and asymmetry of the international agenda which does not include, for example, issues relating to the mobility of labour or the creation of mechanisms to ensure global coherence of macroeconomic policy, or agreements concerning the mobilisation of resources to ease the distributive tensions generated by globalisation both across and within countries. These omissions, in turn, reflect an even more disturbing problem: the absence of proper governance in today's world, not only in the global economy and particularly the financial system but in many other areas as well, as a consequence of the enormous gap that exists between world-wide problems and the political processes whose framework is still defined by national and, increasingly, local spheres of action.

Consequently the agenda for financial reform must be broadened in at least two senses. First, it should go beyond the issues of financial prevention and resolution to those associated with development finance for poor and small countries, and to the 'ownership' of economic and development policies by countries. Second, it should consider, in a systematic fashion, not only the role of global institutions but also of regional arrangements and the explicit definition of areas where national autonomy should be maintained.

The primary objective of achieving greater levels of well-being for the population, as a whole, cannot be attained unless countries take major strides forward in the consolidation of dynamic, competitive economies. Equity and economic development, along with sustainable development are, in this sense, both part of a single, integral strategy and are linked by a complex set of interrelationships. Social development cannot be achieved through social policy alone, just as economic policy and growth cannot ensure the achievement of social objectives without reference to the direction of social policy.

Citizenship, for its part, is not only a right in itself that contributes to people's well-being; it is also the most effective means of ensuring that the social objectives of development will be taken into account in public decision-making. This integral concept of development entails more than simply the complementarity of social, economic, environmental and democratic governance policies, on the one hand, and of human capital, social well-being, sustainable development and citizen action, on the other. In fact, it should be viewed as embodying the core meaning of development.

I am sure that with this comprehensive view of development and with political cooperation, Europe and the South can work hand in hand in order to shape a better future for the many.

Agreement of Political Association, Commerce and Cooperation Chile-EU *

IN SOME WAYS, Chile returns to Europe today, a place with which we have shared common values. We have come from the far most tip of the world, where dawn is breaking at this moment, to celebrate an agreement which will unite us even more in the future.

Europe has always been close to us and today the dreams of fifteen million Chileans are here with me. I think the hopes of all Latin America is here too, and it is the natural arena to which this agreement must be projected.

The agreement is beneficial to all of us as it will improve the access to the markets. We think that it is exemplary because it is based on a common respect for democracy and human rights and must also include cultural, scientific, educational and political factors.

It is not only about commerce. It is more than commerce, even though commerce is important. When there is disorder on this earth, this agreement proves that humanity is possible. In the middle of the storm, that is today's world, it is possible for us to sail in a serene manner.

We can do it without denying our differences, both in the EU's economic situation and our own, and also within our own coun-

* *Speech on the occasion of the signing of the Agreement. Second Summit Conference of the European Union/ Latin America and the Caribbean, Madrid, Spain, May 17th, 2002*

tries. This is the time for diversity and it is the responsibility of leaders to respect and to give coherence to this diversity.

In the past you, the Europeans, were able to unite when Monnet, Schuman and other forward thinkers saw the European Union where others saw only coal and steel.

I want to believe that we can start dreaming from this moment about an alliance between our two regions. The freedom to trade and invest, of course, but also the freedom to think, work together and spread goodwill throughout the world. From here, in Europe, I would like to tell fifteen million Chileans that the responsibility also now falls on us.

Our responsibility is to raise ourselves up to the level. This agreement forces us to work more intensely for a better society, to achieve what you in this old world have already achieved; democracy and respect for human rights but also a social cohesion so that societies can work efficiently.

The dream of Latin America, which we all aspire to, is to grow with cohesion to make a better world.

Chapter 3

Security and Human Rights in a Globalised World

Getting back on the right track *

FIFTEEN CENTURIES AGO, Imru'al-Qays, probably the most famous poet in the Arabic language, asked himself the following question: what do we follow when the trail has been lost? The world we are living in today appears to raise the same question. Where is the road, and how can we find it again?

The crisis in recent weeks has taught everyone lessons. The first is that the 15 members, five permanent and 10 elected on the UN Security Council were unable to reach an agreement to avoid a conflict. We must all assume a share of the responsibility for this failure, because it brings damaging consequences. But at the same time, we must be clear about why those of us who were convinced that we still had room to manoeuvre, before the resort to arms, made the effort we did.

Historians have always judged the results of war by the success of the peace that follows. What peace are we going to build now? How can we ensure that it is stable and enduring?

The international stage offers more than sufficient reason to be uneasy. Today we can see that terrorism is an international force; that thousands of millions of people live in daily hunger; that the role of multilateral organisations is unknown; that the UN Security Council cannot reach an agreement to prevent conflict; that the protectionism of the few is blocking the liberalisation of world trade; that dictatorial regimes continue to violate the human rights of entire populations; and that intolerance is creat-

---

* *Article published in El País-Internacional, Madrid, Spain, April 22nd 2003*

ing conflict within our own societies and cultures.

Faced with adversity, however, humanity rises to the challenge and finds a way, even if it has to blaze a new trail. The most important thing is to have a clear sense of our search. Looking back on the 20th century, that short century about which Eric Hobsbawn has written, we see an era of catastrophe, genocide and conflict, from the outbreak of World War I in 1914 to the fall of the Berlin Wall in 1989. But at the same time, humanity began to create institutions that opened the way to a multilateral, global world.

If we accept the positive inheritance of the 20th century and the foundations that were laid to create new forms of international coexistence, the United Nations must play a major role in the process of rebuilding Iraq. The Iraqi people must decide their own political future, and how to use and manage their natural resources. As one European statesman recently said, we have to manage the diplomatic implications of recent events in such a way that the future will be peaceful and lasting.

Amid the uncertainties, we must push for global integration that is in the best interests of the people, and for a system of global politics focused on the human being. This political modernisation will continue as long as governments respect the living conditions of men and women throughout the world, both within their borders and in their foreign policy strategies.

Making the best of what the 20th century has brought us involves facing several concrete tasks. The Charter of the United Nations arose from the world's political reality of 1945, a world that had emerged from a global conflict. How can we update this charter, and how do we reconcile it with the demands of a different world, with different social and political realities? This is not just a question of giving governments a voice in the multilateral system, but also of including the input of non-governmental organisations that represent civil society.

How can we deal with the issue of an international economic, financial and commercial structure that is completely different from the one associated with the institutions created by the Bretton Woods accords? The World Bank and the International

Monetary Fund emerged from these accords, with the aim of resolving the issues and debates of 1944. But nowadays there is more to it than merely regulating currency exchange rates and trade flows. We face a reality in which a simple touch on a computer keyboard can move billions or trillions of dollars from one part of the world to another.

Can we take on these issues, or will we just have a world without rules? There is no doubt that globalisation without rules will be dominated by the strongest.

In Iraq and elsewhere, people want more social protection and more certainty about their work, health, education and access to living accommodation, administered with supportive, efficient and comprehensive systems. This is our challenge at the beginning of the 21st century, at a time when the market seems to be the great dynamic force behind economies and social interactions. We must be clear about the limits of the market: it is a natural space for the consumer, but it is not a natural space for citizens. Consumers are worth only as much as they have, while citizens are worth the votes they cast.

We made great progress in the 20th century because we learned, as Norberto Bobbio has said, that heads can be counted rather than cut off. This new political maturity leads us to the conviction that we must now combine democracy with social cohesion. Societies in which imbalances and lack of opportunities become the status quo are societies that risk instability, even if they pursue democratic practices from time to time.

Iraq is the starting point, a place in which crisis can be transformed into opportunity. Globalisation will be efficient if it steers us in the direction of fairer, more open, more democratic and more tolerant societies. Now the challenge is to build a multilateral apparatus that suits the 21st century, in which all people have equal rights and dignity.

What is a utopia if it isn't our dream of a better world? *

THIS IS A MOMENT which marks the end of one chapter and the start of another in the lives of talented young people. The stage of your higher education, which you have just completed, has prepared you to go out into the world and put into practice the ideals of progress and altruism that have always been the hallmark of Duke graduates.

Of course, being here today reminds me of the time - over four decades ago - when I came to this university for the first time to embark on my Ph.D. studies.

Life is about moving forward, about advancing toward our goals. But sometimes we also need an opportunity to revisit the past and retrace our steps. You have given me such an opportunity today, and I am very happy to return to this home, a home which, as a university, one never really leaves. To return to Duke University after forty years is a privilege I deeply appreciate.

As I stand here, I cannot but reflect on the enormous changes that have since taken place in America and the world.

IN DUKE, FORTY YEARS ON

The world of the early 1960s was very different to that of today.

* *A message to students at the University of Duke, North Carolina, United States of America, May 15th 2005*

What is a utopia if it isn't a dream of a better world?

Its international structure was different; its technological capacity and potential were different. And it was different in the way people interacted, the way society was organised, and the way countries related to the rest of the world.

However, I believe that, running beneath the surface, there is a deep and powerful thread that links the ideals of that time to the ideals of today.

Then, of course, the international situation was still dominated by the Cold War, which began after the short interregnum of consensus that followed the Second World War. Its defining characteristic was the division of the world into two opposing ideological and military blocks, with totally different and apparently irreconcilable views of the world.

For four decades from 1948, everyone knew their exact place in the world, and occupied that place. All forms of conduct - both domestically and internationally - were conditioned by this overt antagonism.

By the early 1960s, the dynamic of the Cold War had spread to Latin America. So much so that confrontation over Cuba between the United States and the Soviet Union took the world to the very brink of a nuclear war.

However, during those same years, I was witness to the extraordinary progress that American society made in affirming civil rights, led by a powerful social movement and the federal government, despite deep-seated resistance.

One of the first things I noticed when I landed at Raleigh-Durham Airport in January 1961 was that there were restrooms not only for men and women, but also for black people and white people. And that was the same week in which racial segregation on buses was abolished.

AMERICA: INTEGRATING DIVERSITY

As I observed the progress of this struggle for civil rights, I began to admire the infinite capacity of the United States to seek a solution to its problems in greater democracy and greater freedom.

What is a utopia if it isn't a dream of a better world?

America is rightfully proud of a history that has been nourished - and will continue to be nourished - by the contribution of millions of men and women of different origin, language and beliefs, who have found in this land a place in which to fulfil their dreams of a happier life.

This is the diversity that enriches Americans who are, at the same time, drawn together by the ability - so characteristic of the United States - to weave all these different threads into the tapestry of its values and institutions.

As long as this capacity for integration, anchored in respect for differences, endures, America will continue to be America.

UNITY AND DIVERSITY WITHIN THE AMERICAS

These same principles are keys for the consolidation of relations within the Americas. For a long time, there appeared to be two Americas, divided by a language barrier.

Today, we see that this barrier is crumbling and, in its place, bridges are springing up. English is emerging as the second language of Iberoamerica while, at the same time, the use of Spanish is spreading north of the Rio Bravo. Today, we can foresee a continent in which English and Spanish will be lingua franca from the Bering Strait down to Cape Horn.

And this same phenomenon can also be seen in many other forms of cultural expression, such as popular music in which the lyrics, rhythms and melodies of the Americas blend and mingle, without losing their individual identities, in a constant process of enrichment and renewal.

But, across all their cultural, ethnic and linguistic diversity, the nations of the Americas are bound together by the shared ideals of democracy and respect for human rights. And we have joined together in endeavours - sometimes in the face of great hardship - to put those ideals into practice.

The revolutions that gave birth to our republics, and marked the start of our long road to democracy, sought to achieve national self-determination and, at the same time, citizen's rights.

What is a utopia if it isn't a dream of a better world?

Since then, our own experiences at home and the global lessons of the 20th century, have reinforced our commitment to democracy and human rights.

The states and peoples of the Americas recognise human rights as the foundation and ethical conclusion of political action.

In the present global situation, a commitment to human rights demands that we all act in accordance with these principles and use strictly democratic methodologies.

Only adherence to democratic rules can guarantee that violence and abuse will never again influence our societies' fundamental decisions. As the dark chapters of world history and of our own continent in the twentieth century showed, it is not only democracy, but also human rights that fall victim, when this happens.

In this sense, human rights are not just the beacon that should guide our voyage toward a safer and fairer continent and world. They are also the chart by which we should steer if we do not want to lose headway or run aground on this long and complex voyage.

A continent that is integrated in its diversity calls for mutual esteem and respect, a willingness to reach agreements, the ability to put oneself in the place of another, and to abide by rules that are clear and apply equally to all, independent of size and power.

This integration, which we must continue to build and strengthen, is the antithesis of the hegemonic concepts that, in other ages, divided the Americas and caused such strife.

It is the integration of free and sovereign nations, bound together bilaterally and multilaterally by convergent interests and shared values, which should be our objective.

It is an integration that seeks economic growth and social development. It is an integration that seeks to defend human rights and to strengthen democracy. It is, in other words, integration for the sake of a world that is safer and fairer for all. And it demands that we take an active role in the face of the new global situation.

TOWARDS A MORE INTEGRATED WORLD

This reflection on the process of integration in the United States

What is a utopia if it isn't a dream of a better world?

and the Americas leads us to the question of how we can build a world where democratic values and institutions help to forge a global society in which differences do not degenerate into antagonism, but can be harnessed to the enrichment of a shared human future. In the past four decades, the world has also changed radically.

We didn't always grasp the magnitude of the change, but it has produced a world in which there is no longer room for isolationism, a world in which time has been compressed as never before, in which time becomes ever shorter.

And then there is the question of distance. What can we say about a planet that is growing ever smaller both in geography and in human activity?

This is a contradictory situation. On the one hand, it is full of promise and opportunities that allow emerging countries to leapfrog forward in a way that would have been unthinkable before, achieving new and greater levels of development and welfare. But it is, at the same time, a situation that, in the absence of corrective action, produces enormous inequalities within and between countries.

Once we left the Cold War behind with the twentieth century, global terrorism emerged as a new threat, posed not by another power or state, but by networks. That makes it an enemy more difficult to detect, combat, and defeat. However, the historical change we have witnessed runs much deeper still.

Let us be explicit: the Cold War was the last stage of a long period that began with the Peace of Westphalia and lasted for more than three centuries. In that period, international relations hinged on a balance of power between nation states that had achieved the status of world powers.

In that period, war broke out when the balance of power was disturbed, and peace was restored when a new balance was established. That period is now definitively over. And, as a result, we must all learn anew how to formulate and implement our foreign policies.

Small countries, such as Chile, can no longer find a niche with-

What is a utopia if it isn't a dream of a better world?

in the framework of a balance of power among large countries. And large countries have to understand that we now live in a world in which there is only one global power: the United States of America.

That process has been difficult for us all, including the United States itself, which has faced the uncharted challenge of exercising power without another nation acting as a counterbalance.

And it was in the midst of the difficult process of learning to flex these new muscles that America suffered the Al Qaeda terrorist attacks of September 11, 2001. Those attacks made it more urgent and crucial that we rise to the challenges of the 21st century, with initiatives that build on the lessons of history, but also take account of the new shape of the world. As the United States and the other countries of the world have sought to collaborate in combating terrorism, we have had to rely on multilateral norms and institutions that were created in the 20th century.

These norms and institutions, inspired by Wilson's Fourteen Points and, later, by Roosevelt's vision of the importance of the United Nations, were designed to cope with wars between states.

Our task is to reach a global agreement on the reforms that are now required so that we can respond both legitimately and effectively to the challenges of today's world. We do not want globalisation without rules because, then, the law of the strongest prevails.

It is true that the world today is not without rules and institutions, but many of them need updating, and we also require new rules to ensure that globalisation is governable. That is the way to safeguard public goods effectively, such as respect for human rights, the protection of the environment, and the defeat of poverty and of inequalities. And, in that way, we will also be combating instability, inequality and injustice that are the breeding grounds for terror and insecurity on a global scale.

At the same time, we must persist in our efforts to ensure that democracy and freedom continue to spread and take root in all regions of the world, because this is the way to build a world that is not only more fair, but also more secure, for all.

The consolidation of democracy and freedom also demands the

What is a utopia if it isn't a dream of a better world?

implementation of public policies that distribute welfare in each region and country.

That is what we have been doing in Chile by strengthening democracy, implementing social policies and extending the boundaries of freedom. And it is a task in which we will not flag. In his time, the Roman Emperor Hadrian took culture to all the countries under his empire; today, those of us who believe in freedom and democracy must carry these ideals to all the societies of our world. That is possible only through public policies at a national, regional and global level.

Today, integration into the world is vital for all countries. And it must be an active, not passive, integration that allows them to take advantage of new opportunities while defending themselves against adversity, and which allows them to achieve integration without sacrificing their identity.

We must compete tirelessly and to do so successfully, we need countries that are more just, in which there is more cohesion, and in which the benefits of growth are shared by all.

That is why Chile's chosen path has been to perfect its democracy while, at the same time, increasing social justice and achieving sustained growth. Thanks to these three pillars, we aspire to reach the threshold of development in the not too distant future. But we visualise development not only in terms of growth rates but also - and above all - in terms of the dignity of those who have less.

The market obviously has an important role in the modern economy. It is the source of economic dynamism, entrepreneurship and investment, but the market alone cannot satisfy the needs of our citizens. In the market, an individual's value is determined by his or her possessions; in the community, all citizens are equal and have the same rights.

Social cohesion is the great challenge of our region. A country that lacks cohesion and is torn by social difficulties and tensions cannot be competitive in the world. In this sense, our challenge is diametrically opposed to that of the developed world, where the costs of social protection - perhaps because it is so extensive - are sometimes seen as a barrier to competitiveness.

What is a utopia if it isn't a dream of a better world?

UNIVERSITY GRADUATES IN THE MODERN WORLD

This is an age that calls for great endeavours to unite us in pursuit of our shared ideals. Bergson encouraged us to: "act like men of thought and think like men of action". An education, such as you have received here at Duke, helps to bring that difficult goal within our grasp, and that is precisely why it is so important.

Politics and, indeed, life itself is like science. It is a permanent process of trial and error, of success and failure. This is something that democracy, as a form of government, takes into account.

That is why it excludes no-one and allows everyone a voice in public debate and, indirectly, in collective decisions.

Above all, in politics, we cannot be inflexible in clinging to our initial position. Instead, we have to enter into dialogue with those who hold a different view, seeking agreements that facilitate development and preserve social peace. "Neither conflict at any price nor agreement no matter how"; that wise advice was given to us by Paul Ricoeur. And it is the key to ensuring the stability of democracy.

And it is a challenge posed today on a global scale. The globalisation that is taking place today is not just a process to be witnessed and observed; it is a transformation that calls for regulation and in which we must all play a role.

Globalisation cannot be a force that acts without restraint; it cannot be a tide that sweeps us in a direction that we have not chosen. We must continue to collaborate in the task of defining and implementing international rules and institutions that will, one day, allow us to achieve, on a global scale, what domestic law once achieved at the level of nation states: peace, order, and security.

There will, of course, be those who say this is utopian. But my answer is that, during the transition from feudal state to nation state, it must also have seemed utopian to suggest a monopoly on the use of force. Moreover, what is a utopia if it isn't our dream of a better world? Nothing and no-one can deprive us of the ability - the right even - to imagine a better world. Because better worlds are not only necessary; they are also possible.

What is a utopia if it isn't a dream of a better world?

From the starting point of the Universal Declaration of Human Rights signed in Paris in 1948, who would have imagined that, just over fifty years later, the theory and practice of fundamental rights would have achieved such impressive international progress? Wouldn't an international agreement on civil and political rights also have been considered utopian? And, later, an international agreement on economic, social, and cultural rights? And also international conventions against torture, racial discrimination, and discrimination against women? And, finally, to propose an International Criminal Court to try the gravest violations of human rights? But that is what we have achieved in these fifty years.

What tasks are we going to set ourselves for the next fifty years?

It is a fact that fundamental rights are the rights of an individual. But they also apply to all the individuals that make up the human race and are, therefore, universal. Care for the holders of these rights necessarily requires social policies under which the resources of those who have more can be used to alleviate the difficulties of those who have less. For those who live in extreme poverty or destitution, what is the point of freedom of thought, of expression, of meeting, or the freedom to start a business? How then are we going to address this reality?

Human beings must be at the centre of the world we are building, a world that must be able not only to think, create, reason and dream, but also to reach agreements through dialogue. Human beings are those to whom we must guarantee freedom. And we know that that freedom will be fully guaranteed when all our citizens are ensured equal opportunity of access to knowledge. That is the key to our actions, because we know that human beings are born free, but that differences in opportunities also start at birth. That is why it is imperative to have public policies that constantly correct these inequalities and, in this way, facilitate the exercise of liberty.

These ideas will acquire meaning if you take them as your own, deepening and developing them as you pursue the dream of a country and world that revolves around human beings, a world in which everyone is needed and no-one is superfluous.

What is a utopia if it isn't a dream of a better world?

As President Franklin D. Roosevelt said in his speech The Four Freedoms' in 1941: "That is no vision of a distant millennium. It is a definite basis for a kind of world attainable in our own time and generation." 'Since he uttered those words, we have taken vast strides along this road, but we still have a long way to go. And you, as graduates of Duke University, have the will, talents and skills to make an enormous contribution to our progress along this shared road.

Declaration for the release of Aung San Suu Kyi *

IT IS NOW TWO YEARS since Aung San Suu Kyi, the great champion of democracy in Myanmar (Burma), was last arrested. On May 30, 2003, a militia force ambushed her convoy, killing many of her supporters. The life of Aung San Suu Kyi has been marked by the struggle to keep alive her people's hopes of freedom, justice and democracy. On June 19 she reaches the age of sixty.

Her situation pains us deeply and is at odds with our political principles. Her arrest is an affront to all those who believe in liberty, in democracy, in human rights and in the sovereign right of citizens to choose their own destiny.

The military junta that today holds power in Burma snatched from Aung San Suu Kyi and the National League for Democracy their victory in the election of 1990. The NLD won 392 of the 485 contested seats but, despite having called the election, the military regime refused to hand over power and, instead, launched a campaign of harassment and repression against the opposition.

Aung San Suu Kyi is a woman of courage and we know that she will not flag in demonstrating the greatness that the world recognised in 1991 when she was awarded the Nobel Peace Prize. For our part, we would like to reiterate our commitment to continue supporting freedom for the Burmese people and its right to live in democracy. We urge the military regime to begin

---

* *Joint declaration by Ricardo Lagos, Thabo Mbeki, Göran Persson and Helen Clark, published in the International Herald Tribune, New York, United States of America, June 18th 2005*

Declaration for the release of Aung San Suu Kyi

a real process of national reconciliation and a peaceful transition to democracy, and to release the political prisoners in Burma.

The defence of human rights knows no frontiers. That is why, impelled by our ethical and political convictions, we add our voices to those who defend and honour Aung San Suu Kyi. And that is why we also call on other political leaders, intellectuals, artists, young people and, indeed, all our citizens to join together on June 19 in demanding justice and freedom for this great Burmese leader.

Chapter 4

Development, Technology and Globalisation

Public goods and citizenship: How do we proceed? *

500 YEARS AGO, controversy spread through Europe as feudal states became nation states, and certain rules had to be established. Only the state could engrave coins, for example, and it would take charge of foreign relations and defence policies. This was a huge step forward, unprecedented in history. Then along came the industrial revolution, and in the face of major social and economic upheaval, the world had to re-think everything once again with the growth of cities and the advent of trains.

Now it is globalisation that is influencing the way we see politics, economics, culture and society, as this new reality compels us to face the 21st century with relevant institutions, rather than the ones of five decades ago. One could say that we are on the threshold of a new era, which will require a change of rules.

In the great steps forward taken throughout history, it was essential to face new realities and respond by creating rules and guidelines to address those realities, so how will we now react to to the new global reality? Can we create rules and standards that will accommodate relations between countries, economic entities and people, or will everything continue as it is now? Can we create policies to regulate so-called public goods, such as the environment, international justice, human rights, the fight against global epidemics, cultural diversity and human knowledge? To what extent can we regulate international financial transactions, global macroeconomics and financial stability?

I think the time has come to view these challenges in a new

* *Article published in El País, Madrid, Spain, September 5th 2003* way. We will have to distinguish between those who believe that globalisation will bring about more growth, and those who think that globalisation is working against them. We can open up a gap between these two lines of thought. I believe that globalisation is a reality, and that it should expand further according to the wishes of the majority, according to the majority of the world's citizens. The key lies in defining central concepts and a plan of action, and we would like to add our input from the point of view of the south of the world.

According to a study completed last year by the Centre for Latin American and Caribbean Economic and Political Studies (CEPAL), deficiencies in the current process of globalisation point towards three main objectives:

- Guaranteeing an adequate supply of global public goods
- Building up a global system based on human rights. This is called global citizenship.
- Gradually overcoming injustices in the global economic system.

The first of these emphasises new ways to manage the interdependence among nations, and the various other players in this process. The other two focus on equality, both among citizens and, just as importantly, among nations. A theme running through all three is the need to establish public policy around two main issues: a) who defines these public policies, and where, and b) who implements them, and where.

During the globalisation process, many looked to the market, thinking that it would put everything in order. But a dependence exclusively on the market, rather than on public policy, means relying exclusively on a consumer society. What we want is a democratic society, where public policies are defined by the citizens. Therefore, as democracy and its institutions become more entrenched we have to stand by these convictions. Just as this is both necessary and important domestically, it is all the more important internationally, as globalisation expands its reach.

This way of thinking comes as a challenge to the so-called

Public goods and citizenship: How do we proceed?

"third way." In the past, when areas such as education, healthcare or housing we designated as public goods, there were no doubts about how this would be done. A Ministry was made responsible for carrying out the programme, and if no such Ministry existed, it would be created. The State did what it had to do, and growth was achieved. Today, some of these services, or public goods, can be offered using the market, or at least with the collaboration of the private sector. This is not what makes a difference. The difference lies in who makes the decisions, how they are made, and what the overarching goals are. And this is where the participation of the people in the process —both within national borders and also around the world—comes in.

This helps us look at development in a different way: what brings about development is not just economic growth or the influx of external capital. We have to change the way we see things, and this is why public policy is important, particularly in the following areas:

- The way we can incorporate private development funding into areas which have historically been the domain of public funding, such as infrastructure, education, healthcare and even the penal system.
- Defining areas where we can transfer significant funds, on a global scale, the way that the United States Federal Government has transferred funds to state governments for infrastructure development, or the way that funds have been disbursed throughout the process of European integration.
- Creating a more orderly way for developed countries to provide certain subsidies, particularly farm subsidies, which create difficulties for developing countries to compete in these markets. Globalisation ought to have universal rules for everyone, and offer possibilities for everyone to compete. Until now, this has not been the case.
- Regulating globalisation. The current situation, with either no rules at all, or certain rules based on definitions constructed by

Public goods and citizenship: How do we proceed?

a limited number of countries, will be difficult to sustain.

Financial organisations that came into being as a result of Bretton Woods need to offer an agenda for reform, elucidated in two ways. On the one hand, they should move beyond prevention and financial resolution, to put forward special policies for the smallest and poorest countries. On the other hand, a system should be created to define not only the role of international financial institutions, but also that of regional organisations. In this way, the areas in which nations have autonomy will be clarified.

The role of multilateral development organisations in the financing of social welfare in times of crisis cannot be stressed enough. Our experience has taught us that something is wrong when financial crises are dealt with in different ways, according to whether they happen in the world's north or the south. Developing countries generally have to deal with financial conditions that are cyclical, rather than countercyclical, but the US and Europe are not experiencing this. Instead, they are following countercyclical policies and lowering taxes. So if they think this is the correct way to address financial problems, why should different policies be pursued in the southern hemisphere? Instead of providing solutions, cyclical fiscal policies compound the damages already done.

There are countries that still need help to escape from underdevelopment, and others, like Chile, that require fair trade in order to compete and grow further. Countries that were victorious in 1945 have the power to effect change in the world, and others have also emerged with the clout and levels of development which give them a voice on the world stage.

Changes need to be made in order to create new national and global public policies that are focused on the individual. A global system without social cohesion is a minefield for the 21st century, where no one knows what will explode, or when, or what kind of chain reaction it will cause. We have to move down another path, where we can achieve equality.

The challenges to harness IT for the poor *

UNTIL A DECADE AGO, the three of us were partners in a struggle for freedom and democracy in Chile and South Africa. That victory was won in Chile in 1989 and in South Africa in 1994. Today our countries are all led by social democratic governments.

With the same spirit of solidarity and decisiveness as we struggled against and defeated dictatorships, we are now joining forces to enhance development and alleviate poverty.

Our present challenge is the new economy of knowledge and information. With information technology, the concept of global solidarity has been given a new thrust. Information technology is a key factor in all processes for development - economic, political and cultural - all over the world. But it is still only an elite that has access to this key. The digital gap is already here. Our task as political leaders is to ensure that it narrows, within and between our nations.

Some developing countries have advanced their competitiveness rather quickly and thereby leaped into the global economy. But so far most of the winners are Western or Northern nations. This is not acceptable, and we are committed to democratise information technology. This will be at the top of the agenda in our countries and in regional and global forums. We will support projects to facilitate the rise of developing countries to become e-commerce capable societies.

* *Joint article by Ricardo Lagos, Thabo Mbeki and Göran Persson, published in the International Herald Tribune, New York, United States of America, July 14th 2000*

The challenges to harness IT for the poor

We have a common political vision and aim: to create an inclusive and efficient welfare and people-centred society where it may not exist, and to modernise it where it may have become irrelevant and outdated. This can be accomplished only through broad access to information technology, knowledge and skills. We recognise and welcome the potential for development created by globalisation. We want market economies but not market societies. We are dissatisfied because the growth and development produced so far have not contributed enough to alleviating poverty and promoting equality in large parts of the world. On the contrary, they have made the rich richer and marginalised even more the excluded.

The three of us are committed in each of our countries to promoting a culture for learning, for entrepreneurs and innovators. Priority must be given to investment in equipment and training for small and medium enterprises. Competence in information technology must be given a priority in our educational systems, and conditions for investments in infrastructure must be facilitated. We will share our experiences and cooperate to support each other's efforts.

As one of the most advanced information-technology countries, Sweden plays a special role in this process. The success of IT development in Sweden is closely linked to broad access by the population, 55 per cent of which connected to the Internet during this past May.

IT is also an important instrument for the future to maintain and deepen democracy. To involve all people in decisions that affect their lives is a fundamental social democratic task. If we cannot achieve this in our own societies, we will not be able to develop regional and global democracy.

This is especially important since, despite the wave of democratisation in the '90s, too many people live under regimes of oppression and human rights abuse. We who have won our freedom will not forget those who are still struggling. The acts of cruelty in Rwanda, the Balkans and Chechnya demonstrate clearly that the world is far from humane.

The challenges to harness IT for the poor

Social democracy has always been an internationalist ideology, and solidarity must be a reality, not only a word. Today, social democratic leaders in Europe, Africa, Latin America and elsewhere can meet in cyber space. We share and discuss the same kinds of problems, and we are heading toward the common goal - a world in which the success of democracy is legitimised by the quality of life experienced by the poor in the poorest countries, not by the rich in the wealthiest ones.

A view from the South *

I WILL TRY TO PRESENT a view from the South, which is, I think, going to be a little different. The first thing that I would like to say is that usually Chile is presented as a very good student in the Latin American class. We've completed all the tasks assigned to us by the so-called 'Washington Consensus', and here we are. Nevertheless, the fact that Chile has completed these tasks does not necessarily mean that the Washington consensus is correct. What the Washington consensus says you have to do – with regard to fiscal, monetary and trade policies - is a necessary condition, but it's not enough. It's a necessary but not a sufficient condition. In Chile, we were able to stick to the Washington Consensus because in addition to it we did other things, and this is what really made the difference. It's not a question of fiscal policies, it's not a question of monetary policy, and it's not a question of free trade agreements. That is not the point. The point is that in addition to these, if you are going to have growth, you need public policies that ensure that growth will be enjoyed by the many. If not, then you are on the wrong track. In the long-term, if you are not creating a cohesive society you will be defeated. This is what I think has happened in most American countries. They thought that the Washington Consensus was sufficient, and it was not. If, given the growth we had in the 1990s, we were able to reduce the proportion of people living on the poverty line from 40 to 20 per cent, it was due to the public policies that accompa-

* *Edited version of the speech delivered in the Round Table of the Progressive Governance Conference, London, United Kingdom, July 12th 2003. Participants included Bill Clinton, Ricardo Lagos, Jean Chretien, Pascal Lamy and Jack Straw.*

nied this growth, not because of the growth itself.

Second, if you are going to rely on the market alone, without public policies, that means that you are going to rely surely on the consumer. We are consumers, there is no question of that, but all of us display different types of consumption depending on how many coins we have in our pocket. Therefore, if you are going to be dealing only through a consumer society, you are going to create a market society. In a democracy public policies should be defined by citizens, and the big difference here is that we are all citizens and are all citizens on the same equal footing. The real question, then, is who is going to define those public goods that society thinks should be available to everybody. But, the difference is who is going to make the definition - this is what I think really matters. The fact that you use a market mechanism doesn't necessarily imply that you will create a market society. It is who is going to define the public goods that counts. So we have to ask, does it really matter who is in charge, either a state enterprise or private enterprise?

It also seems essential, in my opinion, to keep track of the type of policy in order to ensure that growth will be experienced by different regions in any particular country, and in different sectors of society. The tools that we used to reduce numbers below the poverty line in the 1990s are no longer any use in trying to reduce those beneath the poverty line from 20 to 10 per cent. Put simply, we are going to need different tools in this new development stage. Our housing programme, for example, to reach the lowest 20 per cent of our income distribution, will have to be significantly subsidised - if we decide that this group needs to have housing. The other point that I would like to make is that it seems to me that in this world it often feels as though only two worlds exist, the developed and the under-developed. I don't think this is very fair. I think that one must have some middle-income countries emerging. We are not against development aid. Development aid is essential in African countries, but not as important in Latin American countries, for whom trade is much more important. I entirely agree with President Clinton, who said that we need a trade plus agenda. But, what is a trade plus agenda? How are we going to overcome the asymmetries when discussing free trade? We have an agreement with Europe, an agreement with the US, and an agreement with Canada. But, openly and candidly, in some areas these just don't work. In the long-term if we do not create a cohesive society we will all be defeated.

We had a chat over coffee, before coming down here, about subsidies. US$100 billion is quite a lot of money, and that US$100 billion could be used in so many ways other than providing aid to the cows of Europe. What I'm trying to say is that we have to learn, in this world, what our interests are. And with regard to this part of the agenda, who will be our partners? This is not a clear-cut definition. The other point that I would like to make is that the asymmetries are very large: concerning financing, access to development funds and the conditions that some multilateral institutions place on some countries. This is not the case with Chile because our finances are in good order. The director of the budget normally says no, even to the president. So, we don't need to go to the IMF or to the World Bank. We go on our own conditions, but today I would like to speak for those that, under critical conditions, have no alternative. The conditions are normally pro, not anti-fiscal. If the economy is in decline the recipe is very clear, you have to reduce expenditure. This is not the recipe that the Europeans or Americans are now following; they are reducing taxes. If they think that reducing taxes is the right recipe for them, can they really say to our Argentinean friends: why don't you reduce taxes in order to solve your deficit? In other words, what I'm trying to say is that those policies are pro-cyclical and therefore produce more harm than good. Chile was the only country, given our growing finances, that was in a position to expand from the public sector when the economy slowed.

A further point, which I think is essential, is to realise that the institutions we have, both economic and political, are the institutions that the world needed after the Second World War. The decisions made at Bretton Woods - to create the International Monetary Fund and the World Development Fund – were decisions of their time, and different from what we need today. The big question is, are we going to face up to these problems or are we going to keep things as they are? Is it now possible to think in a Third Way about the global order?

Using market mechanisms does not imply that you are going to create a market society. It is who is going to define the public good that counts.

Last week I was in the Caribbean, and my friend from Jamaica told me, look how happy we are, we left the Security Council at the right moment. I'm sorry for you Mr President he said, and many people have told me this. I have thought a lot about the meaning of being in the Security Council as a non-permanent member. In my view, if you are a non-permanent member you only have one vote. If you are a permanent member you have two votes, the veto and the vote. And this is a very important difference. If you have both the veto and the vote, you can abstain and people will say, "thanks a lot old chap, thanks a lot, I can go ahead". If I abstain, its not the same. I'm not going to be congratulated because my vote is needed. Why do I say this – and here I have to be very open - because I read in the press that Chile's vote in the Security Council was relented because we were in the process of, as President Clinton said, finalising a trade agreement with the US. But, in my view, if we have a trade agreement it is because it is of benefit to both countries, and the question of how one is going to vote at the Security Council should be an unrelated matter. What we tried to do in the Security Council was something very difficult. We tried to present our own view, and our view was very simple, we wanted to have very clear-cut benchmarks that had to be fulfilled by Iraq because we think that the Security Council needs to have the power to enforce the resolutions if it is going to be a serious body. Therefore, I wanted a benchmark with a clear-cut time period within which to fulfil that benchmark. Let me tell you that this was the position of Mexico and some other non-elected members of the Security Council. Some of our European friends wanted the benchmark but not the time limit, and I disagreed with them. A benchmark that has no time limit is not a benchmark. Some of our friends wanted to have the benchmark that had to be met in such a short time span that war was inevitable. We wanted to have a benchmark with a reasonable period of time, so that the obligations of the United Nations, not of a particular country, could be fulfilled.

The method of winning the peace in Iraq is very important. I would like to see that discussion taking place in the Security Council.

You all know what finally happened, but I still believe that as a non-elected member of the Security Council, as I learned the hard way, abstention is not a solution. We are only a small country but I think that in these areas I'm innocent enough to think we should have our own policy as to what we think is correct in the world arena. Sometimes it is much easier to win a war than to win the peace after you have won the war. So just how we are going to win this peace is very important, and I would like to see that discussion taking place in the Security Council.

A final thought that I would like to introduce in connection to the Third Way relates to the United Nations, and whether or not we can have a real discussion that takes into consideration the new realities of the world. 50 or 55 years after the conference of San Francisco we now live in a very different world. The British government has presented an important document about rethinking the role of the United Nations and the Security Council. I think that the time has come to discuss these issues if we really believe that we are going to live in a multilateral world. Why? Because we in Chile think that we must be part of a global world. We have the trade agreements. And because the global world is the way it is, we need some rules and regulations. What about the global stage? Are we going to have some regulations, some rules or will things carry on the way they are today. What about global public goods, the environment, the International Court of Justice and Human Rights? The time has come to tackle these issues. Otherwise we will have a division between those for whom globalisation introduces more growth and those that think that globalisation is against them. We saw this in Seattle three or four years ago.

We think that globalisation is here to stay and should be for the benefit of the many, not for the few, and this, I think, is something for the Third Way movement to tackle.

Chapter 5

New Partnerships across the World

Free Trade Agreement Chile-USA *

WITH EMOTION, we have seen the progress of a ceremony, which will have profound significance in the years to come. We have witnessed an historical moment. Like Chile's spirit, this has been a sober and solemn act, by which the greatest economic world power has signed its first Free Trade Agreement with a South American country.

Twelve years of talks, diverse negotiations, and technical and political efforts have marked a long road that finishes today. With patience, without getting anxious, and having the essential objectives clear, Chile has brought this agreement to fruition with unity and shared effort.

Chile has today stamped its signature and this is a serious and far-reaching commitment. When Chile puts its signature to a treaty like this, it is because behind its name there is a political responsibility, a country's project, a vision of the future, and a sense of trust in what we are and could be.

In little more than a year we have signed agreements with the most active trading centres of the world, Europe, South Korea and today our Minister for Foreign Affairs has signed in Chile's name, our agreement with the United States. We know these things do not happen by chance and neither are they inevitable.

Although we are a country of 15 million inhabitants and we are still far from the largest trade centres, we have earned the cre-

---

* *Speech on the occasion of the signing of the Free Trade Agreement between Chile and the United States of America, Santiago, Chile, June 6th 2003*

dentials of a trustworthy partner in major projects. Our return to democracy has opened the door. Presidents Patricio Aylwin and Eduardo Frei worked tirelessly for this. The seriousness of our political and social convictions has sustained our efforts.

In today's world we do not only compete with vigorous economic policies but also with our sense of identity and our sense of responsibility. These attributes help us face contemporary challenges and implement our vision of the future.

Of course, these issues are important. But what is the real impact of what we have done today? Five thousand two hundred products will now be able to reach the North American market free of duty, as the treaty is signed and when it comes into force.

If our exports to the USA are above US$ 3,600 million today, we can expect them to reach US$ 5,000 million in the next three to four years representing a 40 per cent increase.

The country grows because it is integrating with the world. We will have more employment and, better jobs. But in the same way the country grows because it integrates with the world, so Chile as a country must integrate with itself.

We cannot advance on an off-balance and unfamiliar rhythm. We will be asked at some point as we must ask ourselves: What are the environmental policies? What are we doing in the area of labour? How deep is our democratic system? What equity do we give to the rest of the Chileans? How can we have equal opportunities and fight against discrimination?

In other words, we are also a country that shows solidarity, is integrated, a country with great social cohesion, without domestic conflicts, because in this way, we can compete more effectively in the world, and prepare ourselves for the challenges demanded by the USA, Europe, Korea and the other countries to come.

On a day like today, we are talking about the grothw of a country that will be different, because we have signed an historical treaty, which will help us to develop. However, it is also important for this growth to reach all Chileans.

So the task now, and without delay, is to direct resources with the benefit of a clear vision of what we are and can be. Chile cannot go about the world dressed up as an important partner of one of the superpowers if we have people in Chile still living in extreme poverty.

After signing the treaty with the United States, the text goes to Congress. The country also understands that the proposals, which my Government will send to Congress, will direct resources at creating a more integrated Chile, which is socially fair, will help the 20 per cent of poorer Chileans, and also those requiring better healthcare. Advancing on both fronts, growing with the Free Trade Agreement and having a socially fairer country is, I believe, essential.

That is why today is one of great satisfaction and happiness for all Chileans. We have taken a big step forward towards our integration into the world. The tasks ahead are not insignificant. Success will not be easy. That is why we must prepare ourselves, with greater conviction, to be a solid country, mature, serious and prepared, a country without any complexes about the 21st century.

All of this also requires our signature. As the President of Chile, I will also sign another internal treaty for the Chilean people, with the aim of creating a better country and to ensure growth through treaties which will reach every corner and every son of Chile. This is a signature that I also expect from all friends, from the 15 million Chileans.

Chile and South Africa: Ethical Bonds *

MY PRESENT VISIT to South Africa occurs at the time when your country is celebrating a decade of freedom from apartheid. It is a particular joy to join you on this occasion, which has a close bearing on the ethical roots of Chile's international policy. However, this visit is also important because it comes at a time when your country is in the vanguard of Africa's bid to move towards a new stage of its quest for modernisation and a better life for its citizens.

That was the historic legacy left in place by the Organisation of African Unity, the OAU, before it was superseded by the African Union.

For forty years, many doubted the OAU's ability to fulfil the task laid down by its founders. But that is now in the past. Beyond the mistakes, conflicts between brothers, suffering, excesses, and the acute pressures of the Cold War period, the recently created African Union means that this continent enters the 21st century on the road to a new stage in its history.

Of course, the tasks ahead are enormous. Many African still suffer the afflictions of hunger, poverty, pandemics, droughts, and a lack of education and opportunities. There remain conflicts that call for a political solution, not recourse to arms. I have had many opportunities to talk with President Mbeki about this reality, and the urgency of addressing it. And, in these conversations, I have become acquainted with his vision of the future and his deep commitment to embedding in this continent an agenda in which

---

* *Article published in Mail and Guardian, Johannesburg, South Africa, April 30th 2004*

democracy, human rights, social justice, and economic growth figure prominently.

Chile, on the Pacific coast of South America, perhaps seems remote from the destiny of Africa. But, because of the foundation on which our view of the world is built, we have on different occasions found ourselves aligned with this continent's deep-rooted demands. The first president of the United Nations Special Committee against Apartheid was a Chilean, Hernán Santa Cruz, and, across the decades, our country has consistently supported anti-colonial policies.

In December 2000, Chile was called on to host the Regional Conference of the Americas, a prior step to the III World Conference against Racism, Racial Discrimination, Xenophobia and Related Intolerance, which took place in Durban in September 2001. That meeting in Chile was not an easy one, but we were able to make a guiding contribution to the subsequent international conference in South Africa. In Santiago, we formally recognised the multi-racial, multi-ethnic, multi-cultural, and pluralist character of the Americas as an inherent part of our identity.

We all know that just three days after that meeting in Durban, the world was shaken by the terrorist attacks on New York and Washington. That marked a turning point in the course of history. And, unfortunately, those appalling events also spawned new manifestations of racism and intolerance, particularly of a religious and cultural nature.

I said it then, and I will say it again now. There is only one form of discrimination that we should foster - discrimination in favour of the under-privileged. Progress in this direction requires the political capacity and will to discriminate positively in the allocation of resources. Equality of opportunity can only be achieved by discriminating in favour of the weak, of those who have in the past been victims of discrimination.

In this 21st century, Africa must not be left behind. But, by the same token, Africa must not shirk this century's core challenges. That is where dialogue between continents, between Africa and Latin America, is fundamental. We want a globalised world that is governed by rules and in which multilateral organisations play a key role. It is there that we must define how to co-operate with those most afflicted by want, and how to ensure that world markets operate fairly, delivering growth for all. In a world without rules, it is the strong who triumph, and the weak who pay the highest costs.

What can we do when hazardous cargo is being shipped around Cape Horn or the Cape of Good Hope? How can the southern hemisphere guard against the effects of global warming on our countries' environments? To whom should we complain when the northern hemisphere's industrial emissions thin the ozone layer of the extreme south? These and other questions call for a new and increasingly active dialogue between our countries. And, undoubtedly, that is also the case when we seek new ways to elect the authorities of international financial organisations or design new policies for the Bretton Woods institutions.

Globalisation is here, and it is here to stay. As former President Nelson Mandela pointed out so appropriately last year, refusing to accept globalisation is like denying the existence of winter and, therefore, not wearing warm clothing. We have to work within globalisation, but we also have to make globalisation work to the benefit of all the world's citizens, ensuring that it provides answers for all, and not just for the few. An increasingly globalised world that does not provide convincing answers at the local level is of little use.

That is why we must foster new instances of dialogue within this globalised world. In this context, there is much for Chile and South Africa to do. Both our countries are seeking the consolidation of their identity in today's world - South Africa with its Nobel Prizes for Literature: Nadine Gordimer and John Coetzee, and Chile with its prize winners: Gabriela Mistral and Pablo Neruda. They bear testimony to a profound understanding of the fact that countries, if they are to progress, require social cohesion and a vision of the future.

That is why we wanted to join you on this emblematic occasion for those of us who are soldiers of freedom. As we commemorate a decade of freedom from apartheid, we hold in our hearts the larger-than-life figure of President Nelson Mandela and his ability to look to the future. And, alongside him, President De Klerk and his wisdom in recognising the unavoidable realities of history.

Chile and China look to the future *

AT THE DAWN OF this 21st century, Chile and China are both engaged in the task of building the future. On their respective sides of the Pacific Ocean, both countries are seeking to build greater prosperity on the foundations of economic growth. And both countries share the same core objective - that of harnessing increased growth to the greater welfare of their peoples.

Chile has, from the beginning, attached great importance to its bilateral relations with the People's Republic of China. We are very proud to have been the first country in South America to establish diplomatic relations with China and the first in Latin America to sign a bilateral agreement with your country for its entry into the World Trade Organisation.

I have pleasant memories of my state visit to the People's Republic of China in October 2001. During that visit, I was able to see for myself your country's rapid economic development and how this is reflected in the vibrant activity of your cities and of your people.

Some people talk about the New China. And, as we look at the vast progress of recent years and at the growth that will almost certainly, by the middle of this century, position your country as the world's largest economic power, much does, indeed, seem new. But, from the perspective of history, we see that this new development springs from the spirit that China has shown

---

* *Article published on the occasion of the visit of President Hu Jintao to Chile and in commemoration of the APEC Chile year, in China Daily, Beijing, China, November 18th 2004*

throughout its long history, the spirit which produced inventions that have proved key for humanity, and monuments that do not crease to amaze us.

Today, I have the great honour of welcoming to Chile the President of the People's Republic of China, Hu Jintao, along with his distinguished wife and the outstanding delegation that is accompanying him in his first official visit to Chile and, indeed, to Latin America. Here, we will be able to continue the dialogue that we began in Bangkok, during the 11th APEC Economic Leaders' Meeting, in which we exchanged views about our bilateral interests, the future of APEC, and the international situation.

Chile is, at present, China's third largest trading partner in Latin America, and China is Chile's third largest export market worldwide. That gives us a propitious starting point from which we would like to advance towards a Free Trade Agreement. We are aware that such an agreement would, in many ways, be a symbol. And we will negotiate with serenity and friendship, seeking to lay solid foundations for a new stage in our relations.

Chile and China both have their eyes on the future. Chile and China must work together not only to strengthen their bilateral relations, but also to tighten ties of cooperation and political dialogue between Latin America and Asia, and for the sake of peace and international development.

APEC and MERCOSUR: An opportunity presents itself *

WHEN THE LEADERS OF the Asia-Pacific Economic Cooperation (APEC) Forum meet in Chile next November 20 and 21, it will be the first time this summit takes place in South America.

This means that in three months, the leaders of this new drive towards development around the Pacific Ocean will come to us, in the southern region of the world. They will be here to see us, to talk with us about their policies, and to define the opportunities. The official location of the summit will be in Chile, but these leaders will have their eyes on the entire region, and some of them will be visiting our neighbours as well.

The leaders of the most important economies in the world such as Canada, China, the United States, Japan and Russia, will come to Chile, and will be joined here by a group of emerging economies, such as Korea, Thailand, Malaysia, Australia, New Zealand and Vietnam. Peru and Mexico will be here representing Latin America. These countries, along with Chile and some others, will be here to complete the group of 21 economies, as APEC members are officially called.

Chile's task throughout 2004 has been to lead APEC activities, and it has been the greatest challenge of this type that we have ever had to face. And we have accomplished it, bearing in mind not only the 4,000 or so kilometres of our Pacific coast-

---

* *Article published in Clarín, Buenos Aires, Argentina, August 30th 2004*

line, but also our geographic place in South America, as well as our presence on the international stage.

We know that our assets lie not only in our achievements in opening up to the world - with important advances in a number of free trade agreements - but also in terms of our geographical location.

It is here where we hope that the summit can bring about new links and possibilities for interaction between APEC and MERCOSUR.

We said at the semi-annual MERCOSUR meeting in Montevideo last December, and repeated it in Asunción: APEC will include several Ministerial meetings with important and influential business people from all over the world, as well as high-ranking international trade officials. This offers our region a multitude of almost unprecedented possibilities.

This is all happening at a time when MERCOSUR appears to be entering a period of greater influence and consolidation, particularly since the meeting in Iguazú. This year, both Argentina and Brazil have offered their support for MERCOSUR's decisions and progress. They all know how enthusiastic Chile is about this agreement, not only for trade relations, but for political strategies and initiatives as well. We are certain that if we keep focused on our economies, remain committed to social cohesion, and remain steadfast amidst globalisation, we will make headway.

This is why Chile has shared its experience with APEC, and underlined the potential of these new links, with others in the region.

Ten years ago, in 1994, we joined, as full members, this forum, which has the goal of promoting free trade as a way to grow and provide greater well-being for the citizens of its member countries. APEC is a unique organisation, which makes decisions by consensus; within its member countries there are more than 2.5 billion people, and they participate in almost 50 per cent of world trade. Almost 7 per cent of global economic growth was generated within member countries during APEC's first ten years in existence, which makes it the most economically dynamic region on the planet.

It was also ten years ago, at the Ouro Prieto Summit in December of 1994, when the Additional Protocol to establish the institutional and jurisdictional structure of MERCOSUR was approved. Chile joined the organisation in October of 1996 as an associate member, and has been an enthusiastic participant ever since. There have been obstacles along the way, but we know very well that difficulties related to integration initiatives can be solved with realism, concrete plans, and further integration.

From these parallel projects comes our desire to be a bridge between two economies. We know that when China, Japan, Korea or other countries enquire about our ports, our business environment and our technological and finance capabilities to serve as a launch pad for their businesses, they are not just looking at our country of 15 million people, they are also looking at the immense potential that exists for them on the other side of the Andes Mountains.

Chile and South Korea recently signed the first Free Trade Agreement between an Asian nation and a nation outside Asia. This opened up a far-reaching, cross-Pacific link, and it does not exclude the participation of MERCOSUR countries, particularly the larger ones.

As Argentina and Brazil reach their capacities for producing soya for export to China and other Asian markets, they know that the "bioceanic corridors" as well as good ports well-placed to cross the Pacific Ocean are essential to their growth strategies. This is just one example of many, and it can go the other way around as well, from the Pacific Ocean to the Atlantic.

It was not an accident that the Presidents of Brazil and Argentina met with the Chinese Authorities a few weeks ago, just before this important meeting in Chile. They probably spoke about long-term issues, and probably agreed—as we do—about the importance of a new round of multilateral trade negotiations for global development, especially for countries like ours.

What happens at APEC this year will be important for the organisation's future plans for world trade. We want the World

APEC and MERCOSUR: An opportunity presents itself

Trade Organisation to move forward, we want freer and fairer world trade, and these will be important issues in the debates this year in Chile. The presence of the G-20 will also be an important element in these deliberations.

The advances in the WTO in August were due to the diverse nature of the negotiations. Dialogue among regional organisations will be essential as we work towards a worldwide trade agreement in the 21st century.

That is where interaction between APEC and MERCOSUR takes on an important significance as part of a larger strategy to integrate international issues with regional and national realities. It is up to us to make sure that the increased income we receive from trade-related growth reaches those who most need it. This is where public policy plays an important part in fighting inequalities and promoting rights and opportunities for all.

We are a bridge to South America *

What would you see as the reasons that led to your visit to India?

Certainly, this visit, to which Chile attaches great importance, has to be considered an historic event. It is the first visit ever to India by a Chilean head of state, and it will further strengthen the already excellent relations that exist between our two countries. During the visit, we will be signing a Framework Agreement for the negotiation of a Preferential Trade Agreement (PTA) that promises to boost bilateral trade and will, in one direct benefit, help to increase the quality of life and welfare of our peoples.

But, beyond bilateral trade, we believe that Chile can serve India as a bridge into Latin America, a bridge for Indian companies to develop business around the region. And we would also like India and Chile to co-operate even more closely on issues that affect global trade, such as non-tariff barriers and subsidies. For Chile, India also stands as a cultural reference point. One of the areas in which we would like to reach a co-operation agreement is Ayurvedic medicine.

Chile is seen as an economic success story in South America, are there aspects relevant to India?

Chile has had especially fruitful experiences with a variety of public policies, which have contributed to its growth and development. Its open economy and its commitment to macroeconom-

---

* *Interview published in* The Economic Times, *New Dehli, India, January 19th 2005*

ic stability are, of course, fundamental. However, I would draw particular attention to three areas: the policies that have enabled our country to attract US$55 billion in foreign direct investment since 1990, placing Chile among the main emerging economies in this field; the diversification of our exports, which climbed from just US$9 billion in 1990 to US$32 billion last year; and, thirdly, the development of public infrastructure through a program of public-private partnerships that has channelled US$6 billion into new infrastructure projects, freeing fiscal resources for social programs.

To what extent did return to democratic rule help in stabilising Chile's economic reforms?

Chile took a strategic decision to open its economy because that is essential for its growth. Chile has just 15 million inhabitants and international trade represents around 65 per cent of our GDP. We are convinced that, in this 21st century, countries progress when they look out to the entire planet and see opportunity in its diversity.

That is why we have sought trade agreements with different countries and regions. Experience has shown that economic policies based on the so-called Washington Consensus do not, on their own, resolve the challenges of equity, equality, and social demands. Free markets and the discipline of macroeconomic stability and of an open economy are important, but public policies that promote social cohesion are also required. What we seek, what drives us, is the quest for growth with equity.

What are the specific trade areas where you think that Chile and India can help one another?

The Indian and the Chilean economies are, in many ways, complementary. Chile has carved out a niche for itself as an export of commodities and raw materials with some value added, many of which India needs to develop its own physical and digital infrastructure, as well as its energy sector. And Chile imports many of the industrial goods that India exports today-from cars to textiles and pesticides.

I also believe that there is scope for joint ventures between Chilean and Indian companies, using Chile as a gateway into Latin American markets. Chile's Free Trade Agreements cover a market that already totals some 1.3 billion consumers around the world and those markets are rich in opportunities for technology companies and manufacturers of capital goods and other machinery and equipment.

Do you see scope for scientific cooperation between Chile and India in disaster management?

Chile is a country of earthquakes. Indeed, in 1960, the south of Chile suffered one of the world's largest earthquakes and a tsunami that, although far less severe in terms of loss of life than the recent tragedy in Asia, permanently changed part of our coastline.

As a result, we have developed expertise as regards readiness for natural disasters that I would very much like to share with India. I also believe that it is important that we collaborate in developing the early warning systems that can save so many lives.

Chapter 6

Interviews

We need to live in a world that is much more secure *

CHILE'S CLOSED ECONOMY OF THE 1960S

A few personal questions. You decided to study economics. Why did you make that decision?

It's funny, you know. While in the last school, there were some courses in economics, and then I discovered that it was much better to study economics and to see how many houses can you build instead of deciding who is the owner of the house when you have a legal procedure. I thought that it was much more useful to have some economics rather than a legal background, so that's the reason why, even though I have a law degree in Chile. In the '60s it was much easier to convince an American university to accept somebody with a law background.

And what ideas were floating around back when you were a student? What sort of things were being taught to you, and how did they affect your thinking?

Living in a very closed world in this country meant that whiskey, Scotch whiskey, not to mention bourbon, nobody knew bourbon but Scotch whiskey was something almost impossible to find here in Chile. Only a foreigner can afford to do that when you have a very closed economy. Then what you have is the sense that you can build your own economy in the way that you want, and this

---

* *Interview in Public Broadcasting Service (PBS), Program "Commanding Heights", United States of America, January 19th 2002*

We need to live in a world that is much more secure

is the reason why, during the '60s in Chile, there were extreme political procedures in the area of economic policies, and these economic policies represented more market-oriented policies like Mr. Alessandri or some middle-of-the-road Christian solidarity based on the independent party based on progressive Christian principles founded by President Frei. And then later on there are also these policies of President Allende. But Chile to some extent became a country where all those policies were experimented with, and why was that? Because if you have a very closed country, a closed economy, then it's possible to think in some of those areas and this is the question - why, with regards to copper, our major resource. Well, there was a big discussion, and finally all political parties of all the spectrum agreed on the nationalisation of copper. That gives you an idea in a way of what is the meaning of living in a very closed economy.

Talk to me a bit about how your thinking has evolved. In the '60s, what did you embrace, and how has that thinking changed over the years?

Well, the change is the following: When you are living in a closed economy, then you have natural monopolies in the country in many areas. For a small economy like Chile, 15 million people is not many; therefore, with one or two beer factories, then you have almost a monopoly. Therefore, how are you going to combat that? How are you going to battle against monopoly? It's quite different when you have an open economy and you are asking for a very high price in beer. Well, you are going to import some beer, and today you go to the supermarket and you find foreign beers all over Santiago, all over Chile. Now, that's the big difference. So when you are living in that society, then regulations are going to be extremely important.

CHILE'S TRANSITION FROM DICTATORSHIP TO DEMOCRACY

I'll ask you more about that in a bit, but going back to history-of course you knew Salvador Allende. Will you describe that relationship you had with him?

Well, I was designated by Allende to be ambassador in Moscow. I never reached Moscow. I think that Allende was what you can call today a Social Democrat. He was member of Congress here. In more than 25 years, Allende tried to introduce changes in the economic policies in Chile and economic structure of Chile. He nationalised not only copper but quite a number of industries that were in the private domain, and therefore all Chilean society became extremely polarised. It's true. It was polarised before Allende, but during Allende's period, society was extremely polarised. At the same time, it seemed to me that, from the point of view of the economic policy as such, Allende did commit some mistakes. We have a tremendous inflation and, therefore, I think that this was something that put us in very difficult times. His government nevertheless was elected by 56 percent of the vote. Allende did an election for Parliament. He was able to increase this majority vote, called "majority" but only 36 to 43 per cent but in that time the country was too polarised. Now it's true that Allende was a democrat. It seems to me that he knew that it was very difficult to introduce the changes that he was trying to introduce, but also the political system of Chile was such that it was possible, even though you have one-third of the electoral vote, to be elected president. This is what happened with some other cases.

In the famous words of Milton Friedman, free markets bring freedom. [But] then there was Pinochet, who brought free markets, but he may not have brought freedom. Can you comment on that?

Well, it's a little bit funny, because you have a dictatorship after [Allende], and it was possible to impose some kinds of economic policies without regard for what Congress may say. Now, what you had in Chile was the following, if you allow me to use this in the area of a market economy or in the area of economy. We were citizens over 21 years old, so we had a full command in the area of political rights. It was necessary to take some steps, you know. You had a constitution with a lot of [stipulations] in order to take care that citizens did not to go too much beyond what the people that controlled the constitution said it was possible to do. As somebody says, in the area of cultural ideas [there is a small clique that] has to tell you what are you supposed to see, what you are supposed to read, and [imposes] some sort of censorship. This is not exactly the case, but to some extent there has been some feeling in this connection. In other words, Milton Friedman's ideas, they came to Chile through the Chicago School, and the Chicago School was working in Chile with the Catholic University during the '60s and the '70s. It's my impression that they were able to provide to the military government some sort of ideas that fit to each other. There was a program there, and they took the program.

Now, what happened lately is that together with the period of Pinochet, particularly in the '80s, the world as we knew it was coming to an end. The world polarised between the Soviet Union and the U.S. The Iron Curtain of which Mr. Churchill used to talk about was vanishing. It's amazing. At the worst stage the Berlin Wall was coming down, and at the same time, in the case of Chile, Pinochet was being defeated. Now, what happened with this was that, while you have this case, at the same time the economy was opening, and therefore the changes introduced by the Chicago School according to Friedman's theories were changes that came at a time when the world was also changing, and therefore when democracy was recovered. Then what you had after democracy was recovered, how are you going to take those measures, or those policies, implemented under the Pinochet regime and change those policies in such a way to have a more humanitarian face?

At the same time it seems to me people sometimes are amazed at the way the Chileans did their transition. It's true the transition from an authoritarian regime to a democracy is the major interest. How are you going to go from dictator to a president that is elect-

We need to live in a world that is much more secure

ed by the people? However, I guess it's much more difficult the other transition, to go from those economic policies taken under the dictator regime when you don't care about opinion polls, you don't care what's going to happen in Congress because you don't have Congress; you don't care about anything. But when you go to democracy, then I think that the coalition that was able to perform this transition -- I was minister of education during those days -- has a tremendous challenge. How are we going to explain that there are some structural policies that have to be maintained? But at the same time we have to take care that the more humanitarian face is introduced. In other words, because the world changed, you couldn't go back to the policies of the '60s or '70s. It was necessary to go to the policies of the future....

As I say, it seems to me that it's extremely dangerous to have a general who likes to have a coup, but probably it's more dangerous to have a finance minister that is a populist and probably then we are going to end up with a mess in economic policies, [which is] what happened in some countries in the region. In other words, I do believe really that to have sound economic policies is not something of the right-wing or the left-wing parties. It's simply sound economic policies now took some time to learn.

How did you learn that lesson?

Chile was one of the last countries to have this transition. The transition was done first in Argentina, after the defeat in the British Falkland Islands, or the Malvinas. After that defeat it was very clear that the military people couldn't command Argentina anymore, and you had a transition to President Alfonsín. And the military in Brazil was going down, and then there was an opening also in Brazil, etc. But at the same time, you know, it was a trend in those countries to go back. In the case of Argentina it was very difficult at the end for President Alfonsín, because of the economic policy, to be able to end his term, and he just transferred to the new president, Menem, six months in advance. In other words, I would say you have to realise that the first question is to have order in your own economic and fiscal policies;

second, to have growth; and then after you have growth, then we are going to discuss how are we going to distribute the outcome of that growth, and not the other way around -- first talking about distribution, then about growth, and finally about how we are going get the economy in good shape.

Pinochet's Economic Legacy

How do you think the legacy of Pinochet has shaped the economy in Chile?

I think that there are two questions in this. The first one I think is a cultural one, the first time in Chilean history when you have 10,000, 20,000, 30,000, 40,000 Chileans going abroad to New York, Washington, Stockholm, Rome, Paris, to the Eastern European countries. Either you are a leader because you are a trade union leader, or because you are a politician, or because you are a cultural figure. Many writers, painters, people were expelled, so what happened when so many Chileans suddenly start looking at Chile from abroad, the most important thing I would say is [they gain] some sort of cosmopolitan point of view of what's going on. I remember going to a congress of the Socialist Party in Bordeaux, a congress of those Socialists living abroad. They wanted to be together in Bordeaux to discuss what can we do with Mr. Pinochet and so on and so forth. So I went to Bordeaux. I was living in Chile. Everybody was coming from [all over]. We used to say those living here command tremendous respect because you were on the spot here. There was a very funny discussion, and if you had been in Bordeaux you could say this chap came from Germany, this one from Italy, this one from the U.S., in the sense that their politics had the [influence] of a Nordic country; the more sophisticated, renaissance political modelling in Italy; or the tougher one of the German friends, to say nothing about the French. I mean, this is the reason why people start talking about some renewal in the thinking of socialism. To a big extent this renewal has to do with the way that the left-wing intelligentsia and

We need to live in a world that is much more secure

the left-wing leadership were able [to come together]. So the [influence] of the European and American countries, that's a tremendous impact from the cultural point of view.

After that, then let's go to the second point of your question: What happened with Mr. Pinochet and the economic policies? The way to understand the legacy is after those people that were abroad perceived the functioning of the U.S., the functioning of the Nordic countries, the Socialists and the left wing had some sort of disdain for these Nordic countries, to say nothing about Social Democrats. Mr Mitterrand came to Chile in 1971. Nobody cared about him. The only one that cared about him was President Allende, who received him in the presidential palace and gave a dinner for him. In other words, the legacy of Pinochet is important in terms of making the necessary changes in the economic policy in Chile to open the economy. We used to have 170,000 textile workers, and you open the economy, and now you can import textiles from all over the world. Our industry came down from 170,000 to 30,000. It's a tremendous impact, but once you do that, now our industry is important ... [to] the U.S. so we [can] say, "Look, we already have paid the price of opening the economy, and we are in a small country; therefore we want to benefit from trade." So I would say that the legacy of Pinochet was that through the changes in economic policies, Chile was able to be prepared for a world that is going to be much more open. I would say was that we were ready for what happened during the '90s after the fall of the Berlin Wall and the changes in the global economy.

ON SOCIAL SERVICES AND PUBLIC GOODS

This documentary is about a battle of ideas. It seems like the world over embraced free-market reform, and it seems like even you had certain ideas as a Social Democrat and now have embraced a lot of free-market reform. How do you view yourself within that battle?

I don't agree much with that statement. Let me explain this way:

We need to live in a world that is much more secure

It's very funny that with economics and with Mrs. Thatcher, even though they were extremely successful during the '80s, they never were able to catch the idea of social justice. The idea of social justice remains either closer to Democrats or to Labour in England. What I say is this, because it seems to me that those market-oriented economies normally used to think that it is possible to solve problems through market solutions. This is not true. Let me explain. Since man lives in a community, there are some social services that have to be provided for the community. The first service, of course, is defence. Someone has to defend us from foreigners that attack us. Then you have social services, or public services, if you prefer, or public goods. In Chile there was a big discussion, like in the rest of Latin America, about education, and after 20 years, in 1920, we decided that every Chilean kid has to go to school at least four years. It was a tremendous effort for Chilean society. Four years of schooling, that was a political decision taken by the citizens represented in Parliament, and they decided, look, we are going to have four years of compulsory schooling. Then another president says six years, another one says eight years, and now at the end of my term I will say 12 years. It means that we have an economy that can sustain 12 years of compulsory education for everybody. That's fine; that is a market decision. No, it's a citizen decision.

I was minister of public works, and as such I had to provide water in rural communities. Water in all communities is very easy: You have a company, and the company will charge you, and you have water. But what about rural areas? And what about in poor rural areas? To sum up that program, at least the state, the government, has to have spent something around $2,000 to $5,000 per family in order to provide them with drinkable water. Why is that? That is a citizen decision, not a market decision. This morning I had a radio interview. Normally about once a month I talk through the radio, and I got a question from somebody [in the audience from a city] in the Southern part of Chile. And she says, "Why in the hospital we don't have scanners?" She thinks that she is entitled to have a scanner in the same way that everyone thinks they are entitled to have an X-ray. If a physician says you have to take an X-ray, then you will have your X-ray. And what if he says you have to have a scanner, and the answer is "Sorry, madam, we don't have a scanner in this hospital"? So either you go to the Northern part of Chile, or you do not have a scanner. When are you going to make a decision that you are entitled to a scanner? And therefore to have a scanner is also a public good. You see what I mean? And that is a political decision. Why is there this long speech because I say look, when we decided 12 years of schooling, drinkable water in rural areas, or to have a scanner in a faraway hospital, citizens are making a decision? Water and services are going to be public and therefore have to be provided for everybody. Either you're going to pay for that, and if you're unable to pay you're going to receive a scholarship in the case of education, or you're going to receive a subsidy. Now, what is the real change? In the past, when you say four years schooling, the state built the schools; the state taught the professionals, trained the professors. The state did everything. In other words, to say "I want to have a public good" was equivalent to saying "I need the state to be able to provide the good itself." Do you see what I mean? Today you can have public and private schools, but I can give the subsidy for the private schools as we do in Chile. In Chile, 62 per cent of all the students go to public schools; the others go to private. But of those private schools, the state pays subsidies so that the kids can go to school if it is private and you prefer to send your kid to a private school. But a decision that everybody has to be in school is a citizen decision. What is the difference? That I want to have a society defined by citizens. I don't want to have a society defined in the market by the consumers. All citizens are equal, one vote. All of us are consumers, but our voting capacity as consumers is quite different according to our income. Therefore, if we build a market society, we will have an unequal society. If we built a citizen society, I think that we can go in the direction more to a more egalitarian society.

We need to live in a world that is much more secure

Now after saying this, let me say this: It's one thing to say, "Look, we have a market economy." It's a different story to say, "I don't want to have a market society." I think it is really the big issue today in the world. It's true we are living in a global world where the market is allocating resources, but where to allocate resources in the area of public goods and services is something that remains in the domain of the citizen. Nobody will discuss that in connection with defence. It is not a question. Defence is a government decision. It's a government domain. And you see that, whenever you have some difficult questions in this area, the states are growing and growing and growing.... I think in the long run citizens are going to shape the societies where they want to live.

PUBLIC SERVICES AND THE ROLE OF THE MARKET

Do you believe that the term "socialist" used to describe you is an adequate term or a bad term?

I think it's adequate. I mean, what "socialist" means is the very old aim of mankind to live in a world where you have some kind of social justice, where everybody has equal opportunities. Now, 200 or 300 years ago, the differences between the haves and the have-nots occurred over the ownership of land. One hundred and fifty years ago, the difference was what Mr Marx used to say was the ownership of the means of production. How can you explain today the difference between the haves and the have-nots when you have a Mr. Bill Gates? Apparently today what explains the difference mostly is education, creativity. In other words, if you want to be socialist today, I would say that education is the most important. We have a tremendous challenge. All of our kids go to school, but the difference in quality in those schools is closely related to where they live, if they live in poor areas, middle-income areas, upper-income. And therefore, if you want to have equal opportunities in education, a socialist point of view is to give more resources to those areas where they lack resources. Let me give you a small example. I was on a campaign, and I went up to a small town where most of the people work in the fisheries. You know, we export salmon and things like that. And I told them: "Look, I have a grandson, and my grandson gets to my house and says, 'Hi, abuelo,' and then goes to play with the computer. And I wonder how many of your kids, when they go to see their grandfather, say, 'Hi there, abuelo,' and go to the computer." They look at each other and say, "None of us have a father with a computer." And I say: "Well, that is the difference. Because none of you has a computer in your house, we need to have a computer in your school; otherwise your kids are going to be not as well prepared as my grandson." This ... is not a market decision, that's all.

So what role does the market play nowadays?

The market would allocate resources. The market can also provide those public services that society defines, and probably the market's more efficient to provide those. For example, as the minister of public works, I had a tremendous challenge trying to build highways in Chile, and I discovered with the public money it was impossible to do, so I defined what kind of highways I wanted the design for a speed of so many miles per hour, etc. I did the whole thing, and then I said I'm going to charge tolls for the highway, and therefore, private money is welcome. I built a business in Chile [to raise money for the highways and got] about US$6 billion. For Chile that's a lot of money [for] building highways, and now we have a change in our infrastructure, and we are using it. And many people say, "But how can you, a socialist, put private money in public roads?" And I say precisely because I am in a hurry. I need to build many highways if I want to get benefits of a Chile that is improving. To do that I am using something that belongs to the financial and to the market area, but the service is public.

DEPENDENCY THEORY AS APPLIED TO CHILE

Let's go back a bit in time. I understand that you had a chance to be with Fernando Henrique Cardoso [president of Brazil since 1995], and in those days there was a lot of talk of dependency theory. How do you view that theory after 30 years?

Yes, we were good friends with Cardoso in the '60s. Cardoso came to Chile as a political exile from Brazil, and he was working at the Economic Commission for Latin America [ECLA] in the United Nations, and we used to work together in quite a number of areas. Now, the dependency theory was to some extent an explanation of the world as it was during those days, where you were "dependent" because you were providing primarily raw materials and you imported manufacturing goods, and then your terms of trade were very uneven vis-a-vis those countries that were purchasing the raw materials. The dependency theory plays a role, because to some extent, the economic policy that you can get from those [conditions] in theory was you have to build economic barriers very high; you have to protect yourself, not have a chain with the rest of the world. In other words, the dependency theory was an [outcome of] a particular stage of the world after the second world war when most of the trade concentrated between the Atlantic Ocean, the U.S., and continental Europe, and therefore most of the growth economy took place in another part of the hemisphere. And therefore we were "dependent" of what was going on in some other parts of the world, and we couldn't profit from the benefits of the technological changes because technological change was taking place there.

And here we were dependent also in another area. Let me put it this way: The U.S. economy, Japan, and Europe were complete economies in the sense that they produced consumer goods and capital goods, and the capital goods that they produced were capital goods produced for the factors of production that they have. They wanted to say they were doing this for productivity, and when we had to import this capital, we were dependent on the technology that was provided for the Northern part of the world and not for the Southern part. In other words, I would prefer to have a capital good more intensive in labour because I have too much labour, and in the North they wanted to have a capital goods intensive in capital and not in labour because the factors of production were very different. In that sense, we also were dependent because we were unable to produce our own capital goods. The difference is, I would say, that because we had a closed economy, we were in a situation to produce almost everything, which is nonsense. I mean, today I say, well, this is nonsense. When is Chile going to produce a car of our own? Never, because of the amount of [resources] you need to produce. You can produce cars if you're going to export, but not for the 15 million Chileans. We are going to have our own car; therefore, the dependency theory to a big extent had to deal with a world that doesn't exist anymore.

Does that mean, for an audience that doesn't always handle these economic issues, that it meant that each country had to produce each product? Could you expand on that a bit?

Oh, I don't think so. I don't think that each country had to produce each product. I think each country has to produce those products where they have a comparative advantage, and therefore, when you are living in a closed economy, then every country has to produce every product. When we are living in a more interconnected world, then we are going to produce wines, we are going to produce fish, we are going to export our fruits and some copper, and in addition to that we would like to provide some services, and if Chile has the consent of Latin America in Santiago we are happy with that. We are, because we are producing services for the rest of the Latin American countries, over the rest of the world. You see what I mean? Now the difference is that 30 years ago, because the theory was that you had to produce almost everything, and because the terms of trade were different between the more developed countries and the underdeveloped countries, then the question was, how are you going to change this? In other words, with one ton of copper I was able to buy two shirts. Later on, with one ton of copper I was able to buy only one shirt. So this means, you see, that even though the copper is exactly the same ton, the terms of trade change from one to two to one to one -- that's it.

We need to live in a world that is much more secure

THE ADVANTAGES AND CHALLENGES OF FREE MARKETS

Why did dependency theory go bankrupt? Why don't we hold on to that theory today in Latin America? Why did we move on?

I think that primarily because the world changed in the sense that the we discovered that it was possible to have our own areas of export, if we do the things in the right way, to the rest of the world; that it's not going to be necessary to produce here in Chile products in every area, but we can export some, and we can import the others. And if we were to import, if we were going to have really free trade, we were going to improve our standard of living, and therefore it's cheaper for Chile to import a car from abroad provided that we are able to produce and to export with wine. The question is to discover what are the major areas where you have a more comparative advantage, and it seems to me this is what really makes a difference today. I'll give you a small example: I went to see a factory, and they were exporting fish, canned fish, to Malaysia and to England. In the case of Malaysia they have to add tomato with extremely hot chili. In the case of England the tomato was without chili but a little bit of oil, and somebody from England came every six months just to make sure that that can was done in the right way, according to the British taste. Our ocean changed, and suddenly the fish that we were able to can and export abroad began to disappear, and this entrepreneur decided then to import this fish from Ecuador. [But] we were not only exporting fish, but also the know-how: How are you going to export the fish that is right for the taste of the British or the Malaysian friends?

Second example: We produce the coho salmon... and I discovered that we were able to export the coho where you put it in ice and you take out the red part of the coho to sell to the Japanese friends. They think its red parts do some important effect on the human body, and they sell to the Japanese, and the rest of the coho is sent to Paris. The thing is that the moment you take the coho from the ocean till the moment that it is in the French

We need to live in a world that is much more secure

restaurant in Paris has to take no more than 30 hours, and we do that, and our workers start taking out the red part of the salmon according to the flight of our friends from Santiago to Paris. Okay, what are you exporting, coho salmon, or you are exporting the know-how for being able to send all things in 30 hours? I wonder if I can say this, but the salmon that we produce is different if the salmon is going to America or if the salmon is going to Japan. And we feed the salmon with different ingredients in order to have a more orange or pink Oriental salmon or a more yellow salmon according to the taste of the consumer. [That allows us] to say: "Look, if we are able to do that, then this means that we profit from trade and we increase our standard of living. If we are able to sell our salmon to our friends in Paris ... then we may import some [items] from Paris, okay?" And that, I think, is the new world that is facing us in the 21st century.

And now the question is once the country's growing, how are we going to make sure that that growth ... improves the standard of living of the worker ... who is doing his job in the Southern part of Chile to export the salmon? And this means then that we need to have unemployment insurance. It means that we need to have some social security, to have some kind of pension system, etc. This is a tremendous fight, because not everybody will agree with that. Somebody will say the market will take care, and I say that's not my point of view. I'm in favour of the market in order to export coho, but I also want to know that worker has unemployment insurance. In a modern world you need to have flexible legislation in the area of labour. I think that some kind of unemployment compensation is essential, and this is really the difference between those that think that the market is going to solve everything and those that think that some kind of social security is going to be essential. Now of course I understand the discussion of what's happening in social security in Europe, that in Europe the flexible legislation is not much higher that the U.S., etc. But some middle of the road has to be found if we are going to live in a better society.

We need to live in a world that is much more secure

BRIDGING THE INCOME GAP THROUGH EDUCATION

And with that very argument there are so many people who say that yes, free markets have improved the standard of life for everybody, but yet inequality is as large as it's always been. So the rich got richer and the poor got richer, but the gap hasn't been closed.

I think that the only way in the long run is education. That's what really makes the difference. It seems to me that the correlation between education and income is very high. Therefore, what normally you have is that in the short run, I mean short run, 10 years, you are going to have a more uneven distribution of income.

What I am trying to say is it seems to me that you can easily improve distribution of income through taxes and expenditures. I tax the higher income, and I provide goods to the poor. You can do that up to a point. After that you have to do the hard work, and the only way is to invest in human capital through education. The differences in income are going to be much smaller when you go to Scandinavian countries than when you go to some other countries in Europe, but this is primarily because of education, and also because of the old discussion that you had in the first part of this interview of who is going to make a decision about public goods and services. If you have public goods, they will provide you at least a minimum that is provided and guaranteed, then it's much easier to discuss the position of income after you know that you have education for your kids, you have health for the mum and dad and you have a good pension when you retire. This is essential in a modern society. If you don't have those things, the position of income is going to be not only uneven but extremely unjust. You will have differences in income; that's normal. Fortunately not all of us are the same, we are different as human beings.

GLOBALISATION WITHOUT GOVERNANCE

What do you think people are protesting about outside of

We need to live in a world that is much more secure

Seattle? Can you understand that?

That's another fascinating story, because up to now, we have been talking about our internal economies in our own countries, and we have not said anything about the global world. I mean, let me put it this way: International relations far away in Europe was a process of equilibrium of nations, and the Cold War was the last part of that equilibrium. You have equilibrium between Russia and the British, and the British and France, etc. Then you have the U.S. and the Soviet Union, another kind of equilibrium. Small countries like Chile used to do some equilibrium. In the first world war we were neutral; in the second world war we were neutral up to 1943, and we declared war on Japan after Hiroshima and Nagasaki. Today we are living in a world where, after 300 years, there is only one military power. This is a tremendous change. In the conference in Quebec I had the opportunity to talk on the issue with President [George W.] Bush, and I said: "You are the first president that has the tremendous responsibility of being the head of a country that is the only military power." Now you have at least three major economic areas of the world: Europe, America, and Asia. And ... you have a tremendous amount of financial capital going from one part to another. Who regulates that? Nobody. You have some control, but not all. In other words, we are moving to a global world, but we have been unable to provide in that global world some kind of rules about how are we going to manage in that world. After the second world war we had the United Nations. There was a tremendous discussion in San Francisco, but in San Francisco you had 50 countries. Twenty of those 50 countries were Latin Americans. We have a different voice, don't you think so? ... What happened 50 years later, you have one military power, but in addition to that, where are we going to discuss economic matters? In Chile, more than 60 per cent of our gross domestic products are represented by export and import. This is really an open economy. Therefore, it is essential for us, what's going to be the growth of Europe or America or Japan. Depending if they decide to have growth instead of inflation, then we are going to have growth also. I remember reading the memoirs of President Carter saying that one of the first times that he went to a G7 meeting, there was a tremendous discussion between Valery Giscard d'Estaing, the president of France, and Chancellor Helmut Schmidt from Germany, and what they were fighting about was that France complained that because the Germans decided to fight inflation, they decided not to have growth and Giscard d'Estaing said, "If you don't have growth, I [can't] export [my goods], and If I can't export my economy's going down." And he didn't add, "If my economy's going down I may lose the next presidential election." So there the things are.

And at the other level, where are we going to discuss what's going on on the global stage? What can I do as a president of a small country with an open economy? Well, [I can] read every day the Financial Times or the Herald or the Wall Street Journal, that's it -- to see what's going on.

If we are going to be in a global world, it is going to be essential to have either the UN or some other areas to discuss these real issues, because now the only way to discuss those issues is in the G7, which is fine, but the decisions of the G7 are the decisions being taken by the more developed countries, the more rich countries, the more important countries from the economic point of view. But mankind has a six billion people. How many of those six billion people are represented in the G7? And the decisions that they take may produce a tremendous impact in the standards of living of the rest, and therefore, here I think is something extremely important in the way that we are going to build the international institutions in this 21st century. The United Nations was a tremendous advance, but ... what's there going to be ... for a global world now? What happened in Seattle is very important. The people that complained in Seattle finally accept that they are connected through the Internet; they are globalised also. The question is not to be or not to be globalised; the question is, how are we going to shape this global world, or is it going to be only

We need to live in a world that is much more secure

through market mechanism or probably the political will of those superpowers? This is really the question. And it's my impression that this is a long road that we have to walk. We are in just the beginning of the discussion.

ESTABLISHING RULES OF THE GAME FOR GLOBALISATION

We were just talking about the choice that the world faces, and where there's no globalisation. Where do you see the pendulum swinging? Is the world going to embrace more free markets, or are we going to go to a bit more state control?

It seems to me that on the global stage now you have only markets, and therefore some kind of rules will have to be applied. You have a successful country, then all the financial money would go there. But because you have so much money, the rate of exchange is going to be down, and because the rate of exchange is going to be down, then the country's going to lose competitivity, and probably the money is going to be taken out. Then you have a crisis. And who is going to define during a crisis? Some people in Wall Street, some risk analyst that said, "This country is very good; put your money here," and you're on the upturn. And then they'll say, "That country is not very good now"; then there's the downturn.

I can't resist telling you a small anecdote. President González [Spanish Prime Minister Felipe González] told me that once the peseta was going down, and he called the Central Bank as he didn't know what was the explanation. The next day he has to go to Germany, and he went to Germany, and he gave the orders to defend the peseta, and the Central Bank was selling dollars, dollars, dollars to defend the peseta. On the plane from Madrid to Bonn, half a billion was lost by the Central Bank; late in the afternoon, another half a billion. Finally he has to talk with Karl-Otto Pohl [president of the Bundesbank, 1980-1991], and then the Bundesbank went to defend the peseta.

In short, more than $4 billion were used to defend the peseta. He arrived in Madrid; nobody had an explanation what happened

We need to live in a world that is much more secure

with the peseta. He was very mad. Finally somebody arrives and says, "Mr. President, I have an explanation -- but do you know anything about economics?" "Yes, but I know a little bit about the real world. A woman in Hong Kong decided that probably the peseta was going to be devalued, and therefore she recommended if you have friends to sell pesetas, and after she decided this, well, the selling of the peseta was taking place over and over." The question is, she has the right to sell the pesetas on advice from that, but some kind of institutionality has to exist. Look what happened with some friends in Argentina or in Turkey or in Russia or in Mexico in '95.

Well, who is going to make the judgment? Because it's very difficult. Let me give you an example of my country. We are suffering because now the terms of trade are against us. Copper is going down, paper is going down - that's it. "I'm sorry; that's the market." "Okay, that's the market."

Two, what happened with foreign investment? Well, foreign investment is going down because the measured markets are not very good these days. Therefore, the investment is coming down.

Three, what about the financial money coming down? Well, financial money also is not coming in the amount it used to come. Now it's true - the market makes a differentiation; I cannot complain. We are able to [trade] in New York, one week, one month, after September 11, that's fine. But all that I'm trying to say is it's going to be very difficult to think it is possible to have a global world without some kind of rules about how that world is going to behave, either in terms of foreign investment, double taxation. I mean, all the rules of the game that normally have to be applied within the country now will have to be at the world stage.

What else is the last discussion of the World Trade Association? What else is the discussion of the International Monetary Fund? What else is the discussion of the World Bank? And I think that the time has come to have a global discussion on all these issues - on trade, on investment, on taxation, on financial flows going from one country to another. It's a simple question of are we going to be able to have some kind of orientation, or are we going to be simply taken for what the market makes a decision? And the market does not always make the right decision, as the example of Mr. González explains.

So in a new globalised world, we also need new rules of the game?

That's right. I think we need new rules of the game. Now, there is an effort to produce those rules by the year 2007. It may be that some areas of common ground have to be established. We try to do our task, and I think that Chile has been doing our task, and we have our economy in order. What we can perceive around the region is not very good from the point of view of the region. And therefore, we are for trying to take some measures, you know, what to implement and not to have a crisis in the way that we have now. It's possible to prevent those crises if some kind of rules or some kind of regulations are established.

TOWARDS GREATER WORLD INTEGRATION

So is capitalism in crisis?

I wouldn't say that it's in crisis. I would say that capitalism is going through another stage, from the country level to the global level. And when you go through one step to the next one, then you will need to have some kind of institutionality according to that. What is the meaning of the discussion between Boeing and Airbus, between the United States and Europe? About what kind of industry are you going to have in the area of air carriers, of the new planes that are going to be built? Can you imagine Europeans saying no to a merger between two American firms? That is the best explanation of a global world. The Europeans can say that. Can we? And a small country, 50 million people. ...

All that I'm trying to say is this: Look, there are some particular areas where some kind of coordination is going to be essential in this new world. In the same way, let's go back to the Middle

We need to live in a world that is much more secure

Ages. Before you have the national state, before you have France or you have England, what do you have? Dukes? Counts? The feudal system. And when you have the state, then you need to have rules. Before that each feudal state owed money. It was easier to have one single currency. Look what the Europeans did with the euro. Are we going to have just one single money? Probably it's too far away to think that. But there's a tremendous advantage for a country to have the money that is the only international money that you have in the world. Don't you think so? When you have a deficit or a surplus in your budget, that is a tremendous advantage to know what happened with that.

And I do think that some kind of discussion in this area is going to take place in the near future. Informally, there has been a discussion on these issues that is beginning now. Where is the discussion going to take place? In Bretton Woods. Bretton Woods set the agreements for the world in 1944, with Mr. Keynes and Mr. White [Harry Dexter-White, assistant secretary of the Treasury under FDR]. And today many people probably hearing of the missions will say probably Mr. Keynes was right, but Mr. White was much more important because he represented the U.S. All that I'm trying to say is, are we in a position now to go to Bretton Woods, and who is going to participate in this new Bretton Woods? One hundred and eight countries. How realistic is that? Or probably the major countries, and the major countries plus some other countries. This is going to be like the discussion in Seattle in the World Trade Organisation that, at the end, you know, you have a group of 10 to 15 countries making the discussion on behalf of the different areas of the world. Something of that sort has to be thought of if we want to be able to live in a world that is going to be much better.

Technology is introducing us to new areas that we never saw before, and therefore I think that if we do the right thing, we can defeat the famine. We can defeat those things, and protect human rights but also understand that we need to live in a world that is much more secure. And secure means not only to fight against terrorism. Secure means to fight against unemployment, fight

We need to live in a world that is much more secure

against diseases, fight against etc. And it seems to me that some consensus now is emerging, some consensus in terms of how we are going to keep our environment. Can we introduce some rules about the environment at the international level? And these more and more are going to be areas of international talk in a world economy, and this is new.

So even within globalisation there's tremendous inequality. I mean, how does it affect a country like Chile? Do you feel left out from the process?

I wouldn't say left out, because we participate in the process. In a sense we are part of the world. More than 50 percent of our product has to do with either our export or our import, so from that point of view we feel comfortable. The question is not to be against or in favour of globalisation. Globalisation is a fact. The question is that I wouldn't like that, because of that fact, some countries perceive that they are -- how can you say in English? -- [passive]. There are those that globalise and those that have to accept the fact that they are going to be globalised. This, I think, will be very, very bad. And I think that globalisation represents an opportunity for everybody. And I think that globalisation has arrived and is going to stay, and we are going to be living in a global world.

So what do you say to the demonstrators?

That they are right in a sense; that they are asking for rules. At the beginning the demonstrators were against globalisation. Now they are not against; they realise that that it's a fact. They are asking for some rules, and I think that they are right. I mean, some rules have to be established.

THE ARGENTINE CRISIS

What do you say to those that say that what happened in Argentina shows that market reforms just don't work?

I'm not sure that the situation in Argentina is only an economic one. I think that to some extent there is also some kind of political inability of the political leaders to agree in what are the major areas of concern, from the point of view of Argentina. They have a federal republic, and as such then, this state has also a position to have their own budget and therefore go abroad and ask for credit. And this is a little bit different in our countries. If you don't have a central economy that will authorise the credit from the public sector of the economy, not only the central government but also the other, the provincial governments. But more important, it seems to me that in the case of Argentina, it's also a question that, if the [International Monetary] Fund keeps saying always "You have to adjust, adjust, adjust," and that's the only answer, that I guess is not going to be the right answer at the end.

When we were talking about who is going to classify the risk of the country, the deficit of Argentina is not bigger than the deficit of some European countries. And what happened in Europe, they have confidence. What happened in Argentina is they do not, and therefore it's not only an economic problem. I would say it's more today a political problem.

So what happened there was that they didn't implement enough reforms? There was no willpower?

No, I think that it's not a question of implementing reform. I guess it's a question of trying to live according to your means. I mean, it's like a family, you know. If you earn $3,000 per month and you want to live like you have $5,000, at the end we're going to have some problems. It seems to me that that's really part of the story of Argentina.

DEFEATING GENERAL PINOCHET

What happened to you while Pinochet was the President of Chile? Give me that stage.

Well, I went abroad. I got a nice offer from the University of North Carolina, and I spent one year in Chapel Hill. Then I went to work with the United Nations on a project about a postgraduate training, social sciences in Latin America. I was very much in academia rather than in politics. And finally I returned to Chile in 1978 with the United Nations. But at the same time I realised that I was fortunate enough to be allowed to return to Chile. I was never on that list of those that were prevented, and I have a sense of responsibility of what to do.

And then in 1983 there was the beginning of the protest against the regime. There was some political formation of the Christian Democrats and the Socialists. Historically, Socialists and Christian Democrats fought each other very much, and I thought that the time had come to work together in order to recover democracy. And this was very difficult to explain to the socialist world in Chile. Finally, they understood, I think, and we were able to form a political coalition in order to restore democracy. At the time I had to leave, of course, the United Nations, and I went to the political arena. Well, it was difficult, because political parties were not recognised in Chile.

I remember that in the press Gabriel Valdes, the leader of the Christian Democrats, was mentioned as the "former Foreign Minister Valdes," and I was presented as the "economist Mr. Lagos" never, never a reference to political views. But anyhow, I mean, then we decided that it's necessary to have some kind of opposition to Pinochet. Well, the question of who is going to make opposition is difficult to say. But at least they don't understand that. They put me in jail once, but that was for a short period of time. Then we defeated Pinochet, and so on and so forth.

After that then, we supposed that this was going to be a short-term coalition, just for the transition. But in the process of ruling the country with the Christian Democrats, we discovered, as I said at the beginning, that more important than the transition from dictatorship to democracy was the transition of a backward to a more modern country and to a more just country. And therefore they would keep together the coalition, and we were able to introduce the changes that are essential to live in a better world.

Now, 17 years of dictatorship is quite a number, and therefore

We need to live in a world that is much more secure

Chile was extremely divided during those days. Violation of human rights existed, and to some extent, Pinochet became a symbol of many things in the world stage. And it seemed to me that we had been fortunate enough to demonstrate to the world that it was possible, also in Chile, to judge Gen. Pinochet, and this is what our tribunals did.

Some friends abroad on many occasions told me, "But don't you think that you're going to be unable to do that?" And therefore we had to do it. And I say, if that is the case, our democracy is not working. And I think that the fact that now I have been in a position to nominate a woman, a Socialist and a daughter of a general that was tortured by General Pinochet, as the head of the armed forces demonstrates to the world that things in Chile have changed.

Have you had a chance to speak to Pinochet over the years and tell him what you think about him?

Yes, to the first part, not to the second part. And let me say, when I was minister, he was commander in chief, and therefore on two or three occasions, social occasions, we had an opportunity to talk. I was introduced to him by President Aylwin when I was minister of education. We talked about normal things that you talk about in a social circuit, but we never had a chance to have a more profound talk.

What would you say to him if you could tell him more of your thoughts?

Well, I think that he knows what I think. I had an opportunity once to talk to him through the TV, as a typical type of a political discussion, you know, how to use TV for a political discussion.

So once upon a time on PBS you told Pinochet what you thought. Could you give me that anecdote?

What happened was that I said straight to the camera, to General Pinochet, what I thought that it was necessary to say, you know, not to continue the violation of human rights. I did it

We need to live in a world that is much more secure

with more strength and force than what I'm saying now to you. But I think that was an important part in terms of making people sure that it was possible to register, to vote. And therefore it was possible to defeat him.

When you are living under a dictatorship, normally the sense that it is impossible to defeat those that are in power is very important. And I think that we thought it was essential to defeat with a pencil, saying "no" in a vote. And we succeeded in that. And I think that was the most important part in our transition, that with a pencil we defeated the general.

THE NEED FOR EVOLVING ECONOMIC THEORIES

You were an economist, and now you're a president. What economist has had the greatest influence on you?

Well, it's difficult to say.... Some liberal economists have been of some influence. But at the same time you have to learn that since the world changes, then new economic theories have to evolve. And therefore it seems to me there has to be written yet the economic theory of a global economy. Up to now what we have is an economic theory that applies to a particular country, and what is the meaning of a monetary theory, about the rate of interest, if you're living in a global economy? Is the rate of interest that the president of the Central Bank of Chile fixes more important, or is the rate of interest of [another economy] more important? What is more important? In the past, I would say those in Chile.

... I remember once Keynes said never, never the Bank of England; that what is the most important demonstration of economy of a country is to establish the rate of interest. I remember the last time that I was in England I talked with the president of the Bank of England, and I said, "Do you remember the sentence of Mr. Keynes?" He said, 'Yes, I remember.' "What do you think now that it's an old sentence?" That's it, it's part of history, not of the new world.

175

We need to live in a world that is much more secure

WHAT IT MEANS TO BE FROM THE LEFT IN CHILE TODAY

Being from the left is also part of what's different. What does it mean to be from the left now? What is different?

The difference with regard to the right? With regard to the right, the major differences are, how are we going to define public services? Who is going to provide for that? And how are we going to finance those things? And the answer for them will be that the market will take care and trickle down. Once you have growth, the trickle-down will go to all sectors in the economy. For me, the trickle-down, if it works, is going to work in so many centuries, but I would like to be in a better world now and not wait for the trickle-down.

Chile's socialist leader is betting on the New Economy *

RICARDO LAGOS, the first Socialist to rule Chile since the 1973 military overthrow of Salvador Allende, recently completed his first year in office, amid growing concerns that the much-vaunted economic "miracle" is losing some of its luster. Lagos, 63, who holds a doctorate in economics from Duke University, says Chile, which led Latin American nations in adopting free-market reforms two decades ago, must now bet big on attracting high-tech industries. He's also pushing hard to seal a free-trade agreement with the US.

On March 19th Lagos sat down with BusinessWeek's Mexico bureau chief Geri Smith and Chile correspondent Louise Egan in his office at La Moneda, the presidential palace, to discuss his plans for what remains of his six-year term. The following is an extended transcript of their hour-long conversation.

The economy is set to grow by 5 per cent or more in 2001. But unemployment is running at above 8 per cent, and Chileans seem to feel that the best is behind them. Why's that?

We had a strong recession with the Asian crisis. But in 2000, we came out of the crisis with 5.4 per cent growth, which isn't bad. The bulk of the 2000 growth was in the export sector. This is the

---

* *Interview in International Latin America Business Week, New York, United States of America, April 2nd 2001*

most open economy there is. Exports plus imports total more than 50 per cent of gross domestic product. If the US economy slows this year, if Europe is slowing and everyone knows what's happening in Japan this could affect our growth a bit. The important thing is that we're the country with the most solid economic underpinnings in Latin America.

I've committed to having a 1 per cent fiscal surplus in the six years of my government. Last year, we had inflation of 4.4 per cent to 4.5 per cent, and if you take out oil, it was 3 per cent. We have very low tariffs: This year they're 8 per cent, and in 2003, they'll fall to 6 per cent. Finally, of the 50 largest companies in Chile in 2000, 72 per cent of them increased their profits or were able to reverse the losses they'd had a year earlier. I believe we've done things well from a fiscal point of view.

What can you do to inject new dynamism into the economy?

We have to help the private sector find new niches of specialisation. Computer software and the Internet are one area. Chile has a very high educational level of 11 years of average schooling. And we have an excellent telecommunications infrastructure. When you put those two factors together, you can get ahead in the New Economy. I believe Chile has to make a strong bet on that. We're a small country, and we're very far away from the rest of the world. But in this New Economy, it doesn't matter if you're far away.

Chile was the first Latin American country to embrace free-market reforms. What can you to to ensure that it stays ahead of the pack?

One of the most important things is to work on a free-trade agreement with the U.S. Our trade with the U.S. accounts for just 22 per cent of our total commerce. Having a free-trade agreement with the U.S. will help not only with the flow of goods but also of investment, technology, and information. We also have to reform the state to remove the fat that still remains. Our bureaucracy is slow and cumbersome. I've proposed that we create an Internet portal so that the government and private sector can jointly make purchases internationally. There are efficiencies that we can gain through technology.

Yet Chileans don't seem to share your optimism. Some say the country is suffering a "psychological recession" after having grown accustomed to high growth for a decade.

We're moving in the right direction. We have a [fiscal] surplus of 1 per cent of gross domestic product, which is something few European countries have. We have moved ahead on market opening and social investment. Last year, we grew 5.4 per cent, yet we had fewer jobs than before. What's negative is the unemployment. What's positive is we've had an enormous increase in labour productivity. This is what permits us to be competitive.

What do you plan to do with Codelco, the state-run copper-mining company?

I'm not certain that privatising Codelco would be the best thing for Chile. What we have to do is maximise Codelco's knowhow. It has to become international, doing joint ventures with private companies outside the country and within Chile. The five divisions it has in Chile [will remain under government control]. But whether Codelco is the majority or minority partner in the businesses outside Chile depends on the business [climate] there.

You met recently with Bill Gates and other high-tech entrepreneurs on a trip to the US to drum up investment. What did they tell you Chile needs to do to make it attractive for high-tech investment?

I tried to tell them that there's a small country that I want to see on their [world] map that has high educational levels, an excellent telecommunications infrastructure, and is called Chile. We're opening a small [promotional] office in Silicon Valley, and we'll send our best young people there.

How important to Chile is the Free Trade Area of the Americas, which is being negotiated [by 34 countries of the Americas and the Caribbean]?

Chile's trade is regionally balanced, with around 30 per cent with Europe, 25 per cent to Asia, 20 per cent to North America, and around 20 per cent to 25 per cent with Mercosur. Exports account for one-fourth of our GDP, compared to just 10 per cent in Argentina and 8 per cent in Brazil. Chile's policy is to have free-trade agreements with as many countries as possible. We already paid a tremendous human price for lowering tariffs, so we want to take advantage of opening trade further with the US, Europe, and the APEC countries.

Have you been disappointed with your relationship with Mercosur, the customs union joining Brazil, Argentina, Uruguay, and Paraguay?

Mercosur is much more than free trade. Mercosur must be an embryo of what the European Union is today. We have to move toward a convergence of macroeconomic policies.... We should have a mechanism for conflict resolution, instead of what we have now, which is the Presidents calling each other by telephone to complain. We could have certain common labour, investment, and educational policies. We [in Chile] have to have one foot in free commerce with the rest of the world and one foot in regional integration. That's why free trade with the US is very important to us.

But the U.S. kept Chile waiting for years to start negotiating a free-trade pact.

I understand the political problems involved. Chile is ready to sign agreements. Before going to Quebec [for the Summit of the Americas in April], I'm going on an official visit to France, and I'll visit [the rest of] Europe afterwards, because we're pushing for a free-trade agreement with Europe as well.

What does it mean to be a Socialist in Chile today?

The last Socialist presidency ended in a military coup. That was a failure. Today I am President of a coalition that's much broader than socialism. The parties created the coalition during the dictatorship to fight to re-establish democracy. And then we realised we should continue together to carry out the transition. To implement the changes that the country needed, it was better to have a broad consensus. We learned that there's no "good" or "bad" economic policy. We learned that it's just as dangerous for democracy that a general stage a coup as it is to have a populist Finance Minister. Both things are dangerous. You have to have healthy macroeconomic policies, period.

Back in the days of the dictatorship, did you ever imagine you'd see General Augusto Pinochet facing trial?

No, certainly not. We have to have a political system where any person, whether he's important, humble, or powerful, can be tried. What we've done this past year has not been easy, but it has been easier that I imagined it would be. Our institutions understood that it was in Chile's interest for the executive branch to govern, the legislature to pass laws, and the judicial branch to impart justice. What's more important than the case of General Pinochet is that Chilean society has dared to face the truth of what happened, and that was tough.

It was easier for people to say they didn't know or didn't believe [what happened]. But when you have a document from the armed forces saying that Chileans were thrown into the sea [to their deaths], that's very strong. When they handed me the document in this very room, and I began to read it, I knew I was going to have to address the nation. I respect .the armed forces for daring to say what they said, that wasn't easy for them either. So, I received a delegation of relatives of detained and missing people...and then discreetly left the room so that my advisors could tell them the names of their parents, who had been [tossed into] the ocean. Can you imagine?

We have taken a tremendous step forward on this. There's no doubt in my mind that when the history books are written about this period, the year 2000 will be very important because Chile demonstrated two things: that its judicial branch works and that [there has been some] recognition of the truth. I know that some people in the business world have been worried about this because they feel a loyalty to General Pinochet, whose government returned to them companies expropriated by the previous government. But deep down, they have to understand that such an independent judicial branch is a guarantee for all of us.

Why do you think Chileans are so pessimistic these days, then?

I am optimistic because we were able to do all this [the human-rights trials] and at the same time keep the economy on track and bounce back from a recession. I think things are going well. I really don't think there's any reason for pessimism. We're not trying to look away from the problems, but I think we've advanced. Ten years from now, when Chile celebrates 200 years of independence, it should be a developed country with more social justice.

We worry about the recurrent crises *

CHILE APPEARS TO BE SAILING through the current regional turmoil without suffering many side-effects. This time round, though, it is not using the same Instruments that shielded it from previous crises.

We explore these and related issues (plus some lateral ones about internal Chilean politics) with President Ricardo Lagos.

At the outset it looked -and your government said it - as if Chile would suffer no contamination from the Argentine crisis. After symptoms began to appear in Brazil, you yourself began to warn about a period of 'turbulence' that would affect Chile. In your view, which are the areas where Chile is most vulnerable?

Since the beginning of the crisis we have been concerned about its scope. However, that was not because of any expected impact on our economy, since we have been adequately protected against regional turbulence.

What we worry about are the recurrent crises: Russia in 1998, Brazil in 1999, Turkey in 2000, and Argentina in 2001. It is evident that something is wrong in an international system where we have these crises leaping across the map year after year.

Chile is protected because it has a solid macroeconomic situation, a small external debt and more than US$15bn of reserves - a figure which in our case means that we can respond comfortably to our commitments and demands. Our exports to Argentina

---

* *Interview in Weekly Report Latin American Newsletter, London, United Kingdom, August 13ᵗʰ 2002*

account for 3 per cent of the total; those to Brazil, 4 per cent.

The floating exchange rate is the mechanism that has enabled us to cushion the external monetary impact, and it has moved within reasonable values.

Of course, Chilean investments in those countries are one of our main concerns, but we believe that in this aspect we should move calmly and await an improvement of conditions. That is what we're doing.

Chile was able to protect itself from earlier financial crisis by introducing restrictions on short-term capital inflows. Will it be necessary to do the same, or something similar, nowadays?

The circumstances are different. What we have done in Chile is reform the capital market to make Chile a country where capital flows can enter and leave with greater degrees of freedom than hitherto. In Chile we have 4,000 companies from 64 countries with investments in banks, energy, mining, telecommunications, commerce and tourism.

Why are they in Chile?

Because there is stability, because there is an autonomous central bank, because there is a foreign investment statute that stipulates non-discrimination, so that foreign investors are treated the same as Chilean investors.

What we have set out to do is to make Chile a platform country, where investors in Chile and the region can function efficiently.

Though Chile is celebrated as a model of what can be achieved with the 'economic reforms' summarised in the Washington Consensus, the country continues to be heavily dependent on one sector, copper, where the state is dominant while anothe critical sector, oil, also remains in state hands. Do you foresee change in these areas?

We have carried out the tasks contained in the so-called Washington Consensus. We privatised several sectors, we have an open economy and responsible public spending.

We worry about the recurrent crises

However, as the president of the IDB said recently in Guayaquil, it is necessary to reform the reforms. This means that together with the development of a dynamic private sector, with clear and consistent rules of the game, we need the presence of a serious, responsible and strong state; a state that works for social cohesion and promotes the measures to achieve this.

In this context, there is no reason for Codelco to change hands. It is one of the most efficient companies in the world and it has been managed responsibly at a time when the international price for copper has been very low.

We hope that Codelco will double its value between now and 2006, and that its contributions to the fiscal purse will exceed US$1.5bn. These are key resources to support development in education, healthcare, housing and all the areas where we want to improve the Chilean quality of life. We want Codelco to go international, to compete in the world. This is what it is doing, and in that context its relationship with private capital takes on a new aspect. Regarding Enap [the state oil company] the situation is similar. Nowadays it is a company that, apart from purchasing oil for refining in Chile, is seeking opportunities for exploration in Latin America, as well as in countries in the Middle East, África and the Persian Gulf area. It has opened up, imaginatively, to the world.

Mercosur seems much less solid nowadays than when Chile became an associate. Does it make sense to remain involved?

Mercosur is a major project that goes beyond the current juncture. There is no doubt that this bloc is undergoing major turbulence, and responsibilities must be sought as much within the countries and without.

For Chile, for my government, Mercosur is much more than a customs union. It is a space from which we can conduct our foreign policy with the world, an ambit from which to insert ourselves in global reality from a regional agreement.

Apart from continuing to be linked to Mercosur, my government continues to strengthen its policy of opening up to the world with Latin America as a whole, the European Union, the US and the APEC countries.

You are often described as a social-democrat Is this accurate? What does it mean nowadays?

It is an accurate description, because those of us who see ourselves as part of the modern progressive movement understand that the government's power must be used to improve the life of the people, promoting a fairer and freer society and a more dynamic economy.

I believe that being a social-democrat in the 21st century is to create the conditions for no-one to be left behind, for no-one to lack the opportunity to use their imagination and intellect. It is to extend to all citizens the access to public goods, such as education and health, so that inequalities are not piled upon the same people and transmitted from one generation to the next.

And when we think about the economy we see the market as the great space that dynamises investment and consumption, yet believe that society cannot solve its great options via the market, but through the will of its citizens.

To deepen democracy and reconcile individual liberties with better levels of equity that is our purpose; that is where my dreams and utopias lie.

When can we expect to see a Chile without those institutional residues of the 'invigilated democracy' which the Pinochet dictatorship left behind?

The invigilated democracy has been left behind as regards the daily life of the Chileans; the Chileans do not live in fear.

There has been a great leap in the reconstruction of the republic and the expansion of liberties. This reality must be embodied as soon as possible in a constitution in which we can all feel represented. I have always said that those constitutional binds were intended to oppose the will of the people.

We have won all the elections since 1988, but the electoral system is so structured that 60 per cent elect one and 40 per cent

We worry about the recurrent crises

elect another. The vast majority of Chileans do not consider this democratic, but we need the votes of at least part of the opposition to reform the constitution. The reforms are necessary to make the basic charter consistent with the reality of what the Chileans think, live and wish. We hope that the conditions to achieve this will be ripe soon.

Latin America after the Cold War *

According to world opinion, Chile is an exceptional country within Latin America, characterised by political stability and systemic economic growth. How has this been achieved?

Chile needs to work constantly to open up global markets and attract investment. There is a widespread consensus on this issue, which has allowed Chile's growth rate to double in ten years, among other things. Almost 60 per cent of our gross domestic product depends on foreign trade. Our financial house is in order, and we have tried to create the optimum conditions here in order to attract foreign investment. Thanks to all our efforts, many specialised organisations see us in a positive light; in fact, Chile's international credit rating averages between 160 and 200 points, one of the best in the world.

This has placed us at the forefront of Latin America, which is currently going through a period of instability that we have to evaluate from a variety of perspectives. However if you look at it, it's not due to a failure in democracy. Of course there are domestic issues that arise from an imbalance of expenditure and income, but we also ought to view this from the vantage point of a model that has put economic growth above equal and fair social development.

The Chilean transition from dictatorship to democracy is also considered exceptional. How do you see the stability of democ-

---

* *Interview in magazine Polityka, Warsaw, Poland, October 12th 2002*

racy in the region, especially in countries like Argentina, Peru, Paraguay or Bolivia?

We recently had a clear demonstration of the vitality of democracy in Latin America with the Presidential elections in Brazil. There was an enthusiastic turnout for an election that the entire world observed, although not everyone understands how Brazilian politics works, or how Brazil's political leadership has matured in recent years. I will say, however, that economic and social discontentment has spread in many countries here, and to some extent, this threatens the legitimacy of democracies on the continent.

Latin America is going through a critical time and it has to learn how to open itself up to increasing globalisation and also renew its faith in, and commitment to, politics and democracy. We need to integrate ourselves into a modern world, as part of a common project similar to what happened during our independence 200 years ago, and create fairer, more socially integrated and more solidly democratic societies.

The economic situation in Latin America is going through a difficult period, due to the crisis in Mexico and Argentina. There is less foreign investment directed at Latin America than was hoped for, and the continent is viewed as a totality. To what extent is this a fair view of the continent, and what is Chile's role in all this?

Two things. First, I think we are going through a regressive period in terms of international investment, as part of a cycle that will eventually hit an upturn. When that happens, Chile wants to be at the forefront of that re-activation. The second thing is that unlike the so-called "tequila effect," or the "tango effect," international investors have shown a great ability to differentiate between one country and another.

But there's something else to it as well. Ever since the 1980s, before the end of the Cold War, the countries in our region followed the directives of the "Washington Consensus." We reformed our economies to achieve macroeconomic equilibrium, we opened up our markets, we recognised the role of the private sector as the engine of economic progress. Latin America made a huge effort to be included in the new globalisation process. But we have to admit that the results have been weak and discouraging. I think that the problem can be summed up by saying that the economic policies of the Washington Consensus were not sufficient to achieve equity and equal opportunity—without which, societal cohesion is impossible—on their own. That is where we have to intervene with the right public policies. We need the international financial organisations to understand the importance of these public policies and the costs they involve.

Since the dictatorship in Chile ended, the number of people living in poverty has been halved, but income differences between rich and poor remained unchanged. Is this a result of Chile's liberalised economy?

The priorities of the country changed when we returned to democracy. Aside from institutionalising human rights and guaranteeing democracy, the Concertation Governments have put as much emphasis on social justice—especially for those with the most need—as they have on economic policy. For example, over the last decade, the minimum wage has increased by 80 per cent, and 30 per cent of all housing in the country has been built. Spending on healthcare has been doubled, and spending on education has increased by almost 120 per cent. Chile's public infrastructure is also about to take a great step forward. But this work requires a focus on the poor, because the market on its own will not solve these problems. The market produces consumers, while democracy is built with citizens. These citizens are the ones who should fight for public policy to lessen the gap between rich and poor.

Left-wing critics of the Chilean transition say that the Concertation coalition in power in Chile since 1989 continues the socio-economic models of the dictatorship, the only differ-

ence being that they do not violate human rights. Meanwhile, the right-wing opposition in Chile sees a return to socialism at every turn. What's going on here?

Both positions are extremely ideological, and ignore the challenges of today's world. Neither an all-encompassing State apparatus, nor extreme market liberalism, such as occurred in Chile during the military government, allow for the conditions necessary to produce a healthy and sustainable development. Economic orthodoxy is not the answer for an economy focused on the person. We consider market relations and productive growth to be a platform for increasing social action to change the way of life in this country. Over the years, we've shown that we can govern the market in a stable, efficient way, maintaining growth and opening up opportunities for everyone.

But the most important thing, what makes the difference, is that the governing coalition is a progressive one, with an emphasis on ethics in its policies and initiatives, including the socio-economic ones. That is our focus, our model; that's how we gain credibility.

When you took over as President, you expressed great hope for the integration of Latin America, especially with MERCOSUR countries. The hope was that with one voice, you would be heard. However, the integration of countries like Argentina and Brazil with Chile seems a rather distant possibility. In your opinion, is this integration still a feasible goal?

It still is, because integration can be done on many levels. True, things are a bit slow now in MERCOSUR, especially given the crisis in Argentina. But that's not the only reason. The problem is that the right mechanisms need to be put in place so that we can coordinate macroeconomic policy, some kind of Maastrich treaty which envisions a certain range of monetary fluctuations and sets limits on public deficits. We are working on this, but we have to look at it as a strategic political project.

Two years ago, to celebrate 500 years since the foundation of Brazil, there was a South American Summit to define an infrastructure development program. Two months ago, in 2002, the South American Presidents met, once again, to obtain an update on this project. There are 162 integration projects in various stages of development, at a combined cost of 25 billion US dollars. Do you know what this could mean? I think that it's important to recognise that in Latin America, and specific areas of it such as South America, we are laying the groundwork for integration in the 21st century.

In Chile, divisions are increasing within two evenly-matched blocks: the centre-left and the opposition right. The slogan "Change" was very popular in the last election. What is your opinion on this? Would an eventual change in the balance of power in Chile confirm the country's stability, or would the system be put in some kind of jeopardy?

Public opinion polls have shown that the Concertation for Democracy has the support of more than 50 per cent of Chileans. Therefore, there are not two equal coalitions here. This is something that is rarely seen in contemporary democracy: after more than ten years in power, a political coalition retains the support of the people. As every election between 1990 and the present day has shown, Chileans have clearly opted for freedom, tolerance, stability, progress and social justice, values that the Concertation and all parties within it espouses.

The Concertation works to bring Chile toward greater development, justice and peace, with opportunities and a decent quality of life for all, whatever their social origins, ideology or religious beliefs. Chileans can see this. A great majority of people do not look back fondly upon the authoritarian past; they value what they have achieved in democracy and have great hope for the future. In a few more months, we will be a partner of the European Union, and we will probably have signed a Free Trade Agreement with the US, just like the ones we have already signed with Canada and Mexico. By opening up to the world like this, Chile will come ever closer to its goal of being a developed country by its Bicentennial, in 2010.

Latin America is a place where the US and the EU are rivals. Do you think that the end of the Cold War, and the recent War on Terror, will lessen Washington's interest in Latin America? How do you see the progression of these relations?

Currently, the centres of global power are beyond Latin America. However, history has shown us that Inter-American relations are constantly in flux, passing through periods of great cooperation, distance, and even tension. Chile's dialogue with the US is very dynamic.

We think, and hope, that Washington will always prioritise the recognition of and respect for democracy, freedom, equality and human rights as the basic tenets of our relations with them, given our shared cultural and political emphasis.

In today's globalised world, with its great opportunities and challenges, both Europe and the United States now value the part that Latin America has played in the stability of international affairs since the Cold War. In the future, this will strengthen our relations with these two important centres of world politics.

We are planning... 5 per cent growth in GDP *

How would you describe what has happened to the economy in Chile?

We are a country that is extremely open to international trade. More than 60 per cent of our gross domestic product is imports less exports. So we depend much on exchange and what's going on in the rest of the world. Fortunately, we have a rather well-balanced geographical distribution of our trade with Europe, with the United States and with Asia. Lastly, with the countries of the Americas, of course. A significant quantity. And this is this reason why our tariffs are extremely low: 6 per cent flat for everything.

Is that falling further?

That is decreasing. And this is the reason why we have been pursuing trade agreements with so much interest. We now have trade agreements with Canada, with Mexico, with most of the countries of the Americas. And, of course, with Europe. Also with the United States, which is keenly important for us, and with South Korea.

We have had a goal the last few years of more than 12 per cent growth in exports. And in terms of our gross domestic product, we are planning this year to have growth of 3.5 per cent. We have an autonomous monetary policy. We have a very good manage-

---

* *Interview by Herbert Klein, editor-in-chief of Copley Newspapers, published in San Diego Union-Tribune and others, California, United States of America, April 20th 2003. Title by the editor.*

ment of our fiscal account. We have a deficit of 0.5 per cent, a very small deficit.

I saw the banks just got a $4 billion loan.

Oh yes. The country risk is the smallest of all the American economies. We have a very good (credit) standing on Wall Street. And at the same time we have been able to make important progress in the areas of health and education. Now we are going for a minimum third year (of high school) education for everybody. It's enforced. On average, our kids now go to school for 11.5 years. And at the same time we have been able to reduce the proportion of people in Chile living under the poverty line from 40 per cent to 20 per cent. Our approach for those who are extremely poor is not to give them money but to help them to get on their own feet. To teach them, give them on-the-job training, schooling for their kids. We have a very good program in terms of housing.

I don't know if you know Jack Kemp, a statesman in the United States. He's a very strong advocate of that kind of housing. To have public housing and then sell it to individuals. Is that what you're doing?

We provide what we call social housing, housing for those that need it. Depending upon the size of the house, the government will provide the money and a private contractor will build it.

With the idea that if you own it you'll keep it up?

Oh yes, of course. And now those new areas that we have been able to do that are provided with nurseries, schools, things like that. That's provided by the government.

What is the poverty line in dollars?

I would say it is the equivalent in purchasing power of something like $300.

What do you envision the rate of growth in Chile's economy will be by the time you leave office?

We are planning to have at least 5 per cent growth in GDP.

We are planning... 5 per cent growth in GDP

Investment and trade are bringing in more investment capital. And in addition to our trade agreements, we have been able to arrange a double-taxation agreement with the major European powers. So that if you come to Chile, if you invest in Chile and from Chile you're going to invest in a country that's in the Americas, then the profits in both of their countries are not going to pay taxes in Chile. So we perceive of ourselves like a partner to the rest of the American countries.

Argentina, with its rich heritage is faltering and yet you have come up to the level where you are now.

Yes. For the first time, everybody has agreed that the only way to have progress is to be able to accept the challenge of competing in the world. We are going to be living in a global world. And that is why we are producing salmon for the United States and for the Europeans and for the Japanese people. And we are second only to Norway. We're trying to produce some wine, not to compete with Californian wines, but to add some wines.

To sustain this growth that you're talking about, besides trade agreements what other elements will you need?

In addition to those trade agreements, we should impose a more flexible labour legislation. We were able to introduce an unemployment insurance, privately run. And that's very important because we have quite a number of temporary workers because of our agriculture. People who normally will work for six, eight months to pick crops. So now these people for the first time will have unemployment benefits.

How do you do that privately?

You put a little percentage of your salary, then the government will put in a little bit. But the money that you have is run privately.

Sort of the way Chile handles its Social Security program?

Yes but it's run by the private sector, not by the public. And from our point of view, this was very important.

It looks like the trade agreement between Chile and the United

We are planning... 5 per cent growth in GDP

States may be at risk of not being ratified in the US Congress because of Chile's opposition to the United States going to war with Iraq. What would that do to the relationship between our two countries?

Well, I think the trade agreement is good for both countries. And good partners have to be able to be very open and very frank with each other. And I explained this to President Bush. I felt it was possible to have a bench mark to be fulfiled by Saddam Hussein in a three-week period. If this were not met, then you would have to use force. Later, I discovered that apparently there were some elements linked to the defence policy of the United States that the war had to start on a particular day so that the three-week period was too much. We had a long talk with British Prime Minister Tony Blair on how to present things to get a majority in the Security Council. And I thought that it was possible to get the majority through our ideas. Unfortunately, that was not the case. We worked very hard with Prime Minister Blair.

But not with the United States?

Now with United States I hope that they will understand the reasons in this particular case. All political parties in Chile were in favour of our position. Now, to answer your question, I think that we may lose some votes (in the American Congress) but I still think that it is very important to pass the agreement for Chile and for the United States. We are not an economic superpower, of course, but I think that it's a very important thing from the point of view of the United States in relation to Latin America. I was talking this morning with President Fox on this issue. Mexico and Chile are in the same position in regard to the situation in Iraq. And I think that if the trade agreement is approved by the U.S. Congress it is going to be a very important message to the other American countries. We've worked so hard on this agreement that I think it would be a tremendous disappointment if the agreement were not passed. Clearly, I don't think that is going to happen. I hope that the war is going to be over very soon and therefore by the end of May or June that the agreement may be taken to the U.S. Congress.

Do you have any signals that the United States may delay it?

No, because we keep working on that agreement very hard. Now the agreement is in legal terms. It's on the Internet. And now it's being translated to Spanish because the agreement is in English.

Have labour unions taken a stand on this issue?

Our trade union movement is in favour of the agreement, which is very interesting. I remember President Bush told me once how did you get that (union support) and I said I didn't get that, they realised that this is important from the point of view of the Chilean economic growth. The majority of the workers in Chile are in favour.

A good part of a trade agreement with Chile is about agriculture and seafood, is it not?

Still, in the area of agriculture it is going to be very difficult for our farmers to compete with the wheat that is coming from the United States, for instance, given the subsidy system that you have in your own agriculture. But at the end, it's true that you're going to destroy some jobs but you are going to create more jobs than the ones you destroyed.

From the reading of your ambassador in Washington, how much animosity did your stand on Iraq generate among the American people?

I don't think too much because I think that our position was a very balanced position because we were against the French position. I said I wanted a bench mark with a date. And if you don't have a date – French President Jacques Chirac didn't want to have a date. I said if he would have a bench mark without a date then the U.N. resolution wasn't going to be respected. And with this kind of bench mark, with Dr. Hans Blix with the inspectors, he said he could question 30 scientists. So I hope that our American friends will understand that what we were trying to do was to present a very balanced position vis-a-vis the position of the US and the UK on the one hand and Germany, France and Russia on the other.

What is your view on the war with Iraq?

I understand that there is going to be a time where the security forces that belong to the coalition will have to remain there. And I think that after the security questions are tackled in the right way, there will be some kind of opportunity for the coalition and the United Nations to have some kind of agreement on trying to form a future government. And I think that President Bush has been expressive in his views and I think this is very important.

So you're in favour of the coalition taking the lead and then turning to the United Nations?

For a very practical reason. The coalition is in the field and they have to respond from the point of view of security. And therefore it will take some time after some kind of international involvement or whatever you want to call it is able to take care of that. But at the end everybody agreed that it's up to the Iraqi people to decide what kind of government they are going to have. And this I think is important because this is the moral persuasion that the Americans have to make to the world. Why they did what they did. What President Bush keeps saying, 'that we are not conquerors,' and that's important. This is something that I think President Bush was very courageous when he decided to go to the UN and to present the case to the UN And I think that if we are thinking in terms of what to do after the war, I think that you should have some kind of multilateral agreement.

Under your proposal to give the inspectors an additional three weeks, what would have happened if they did not find weapons of mass destruction?

For a particular country to have the weapons of mass destruction cannot be accepted by the civilised community. Therefore, the international community had the right to use force. And if Iraq had not met the bench mark, then it would have been necessary to use force. And I put that in my statement.

From your point of view, the quicker we get the trade agreement approved the better?

I think so. In this century you will have major trading blocs. Here you have the Americas, here you have Europe, and you even have something in Asia. The United States already has an agreement with Canada and with Mexico.

It has been quite a long road to achieving a trade agreement, hasn't it?

Yes. We started with Bush's father.

Are you negotiating agreements with other countries?

We are starting negotiations now with Singapore and New Zealand. The three of us: Singapore, New Zealand and Chile. And the prime minister of Australia was optimistic it might be able to join and make the negotiations for four countries, instead of three.

As the leader of a small country, you mentioned that you have talked to President Fox of Mexico this morning. You talked to President Bush at least twice during the negotiations. How do you enjoy such prominence?

What normally happens is that once you are on the Security Council, you end up talking with almost everybody.

Chilean model *

CHILE, THIS YEAR'S APEC HOST, shows how a small economy can not only survive but be globally competitive, as it strengthens ties with Asia – its largest export destination

A farmer's son, President Ricardo Lagos, 66, studied economics and law at Universidad de Chile and went on to earn a PhD in Economics from North Carolina's Duke University in the US. At his alma mater, he was a professor of economics.

Lagos played a prominent role in the struggle to reinstate democracy in Chile. In September 1986, a few hours after an assassination attempt on right-wing dictator General Augusto Pinochet, Lagos was arrested, only to be released 19 days later, following an intense international campaign for his release. In 1990, he was appointed Education Minister and, between 1994 and 1998, he served as Minister for Public Works. He resigned from the Cabinet to launch his presidential campaign. He was elected in a run-off ballot in January 2000 as a candidate for the left-wing alliance Con-certacion de Partidos por la Democracia, which includes the Christian Democrats, Party for Democracy, Socialist Party and the Radical Socialist Democratic Party. The coalition has governed Chile since 1990, when democracy was restored. The Chilean system provides for a single six-year term for the President. Lagos' term runs out in March 2006. He spoke to Asia Inc for 55 minutes at the Palace La Moneda in Santiago. The following are excerpts from the interview:

As chairman of the APEC 2004 Senior Officials' Meetings what do you see as the main objectives of the APEC Summit this year?

---

* *Interview in monthly magazine ASIA INC, Singapore, Singapore, November 2004*

Chilean Model

We have proposed this year's APEC slogan: 'One Community, Our Future.' In today's interconnected world, geographical distance means much less than what it used to some years ago. Suddenly, we discovered that the huge Pacific Ocean that once separated Asia from the West Coast of the Americas is actually something that connects us. It is no longer seen as a sea that divides the people on both sides but, really, a bridge that links our people. In the past 15 years, we have seen a huge change with trade flows that used to be in the North Atlantic now mainly concentrated in the Pacific region. Once we realise that it is in the Pacific where most of the world's trade is going to take place, then it becomes easier for us to promote among ourselves better economic relations, trade and investments.

I also believe APEC will be a good forum to push further cooperation in a multilateral trade system through the World Trade Organisation. So, WTO will be an issue that APEC leaders will talk about this year. It's not going to be a big step but we have learnt that it isn't about big steps, but about continuity of taking small steps and moving forward.

APEC is in its 15th year. Has APEC made sufficient progress in promoting free and open trade?

I think, 10 years ago, most of the fear was, 'How are we going to dismantle our trade barriers without hurting ourselves?' Countries began making advances unilaterally. In our case, Chile used to have trade barriers with minimum protective tariff rates of [a flat] 11 per cent. In 1995, we decided unilaterally to reduce those tariffs by 1 per cent a year over five years to just 6 per cent, which we have now. In the last five years, many APEC countries have decided that maybe they should have bilateral or trilateral agreements like the FTAs, or free trade agreements. Two years ago, Chile signed a trade agreement with South Korea. We are now discussing FTAs with Singapore and New Zealand. We are planning open negotiations f or FTAs with China. We have one with the US which came into effect last year. We already had FTAs with Canada and Mexico. So, for Chile, FTAs have been a step forward. We are not the only ones doing FTAs. Mexico has an FTA with Japan; Singapore has an FTA with New Zealand and Australia. ASEAN countries are moving closer with their own FTAs for a common market of sorts. The world has moved from reducing unilateral tariffs to promote trade, to bilateral and multilateral agreements among themselves in order to speed up the process of liberalisation.

Chile was the first Latin American country to sign an FTA with an Asian country — South Korea. How have FTAs helped Chile enhance trade? What is the rationale for FTAs with Asian countries? Can other Latin American countries learn from Chile in this area?

FTAs are not easy, especially for developing countries. When we first wanted one with South Korea, our manufacturers were uneasy because they didn't understand how they would compete against the Koreans but our farmers were happy because they knew that our fish, fruits and wines would find new markets in Korea. When we initiated FTA talks with New Zealand, it was exactly the reverse. Our manufacturers were happy they could sell textiles to New Zealanders but our farmers thought they would be overwhelmed by dairy farmers from New Zealand. There is a lot of compromise and balancing to do but, in the end, we must see whether, overall, the country gains from the FTA. Because of the FTAs, we have been able to grow our trade with North America, Europe, Korea substantially. But FTAs are not a solution to all our problems. We still need multilateral agreements like the next round of WTO, or the Doha Round, to succeed.

Can APEC help in expediting a multilateral trade agreement like the Doha Round?

The beauty of APEC is that when we are alone as leaders, without the press, with-out the officials, we always have very friendly and cordial discussions among ourselves. At the last APEC leaders' lunch in Bangkok, I said to the other leaders: 'Look, here we are, leaders of Asia-Pacific economies, with diverse economies and some of the most powerful as well as fastest-growing economies in the world gathered in the room. Why don't we cooperate in Geneva, in WTO, as a formal APEC council?' The idea was to use APEC to enhance free trade globally. In agriculture, for example, we will have problems with Europe in the multilateral round but, within APEC, we are in good company with our friends in Australia and New Zealand. My own impression is that through APEC, we are in a particularly good position to discuss in an open way different roads to open up further the multilateral process. I believe that at the upcoming APEC summit, these will be some of the issues we will talk about. With so many FTAs within APEC as well as between APEC and non-APEC countries, what happens to the multilateral round? How do we get the Doha Round moving again? APEC has a big role to play here precisely because our economies are so diverse, precisely because we are not a political bloc but a grouping of economies to increase trade [and] investments and which are keen to implement policies that improve the wellbeing of our people.

To many people, APEC is just a talk shop where leaders get together once a year and wear funny shirts. Is APEC still relevant in this day and age?

As I said, I believe APEC is more relevant today than it was when the idea for an Asia-Pacific grouping was first discussed. True, the grouping is now very large, with Russia, all the East Asian countries, Australia, New Zealand and North America and Pacific economies like Chile and Peru, but changes in the Pacific region have been so rapid that we need to cooperate even more today than before. Take China, an increasingly large economy that is a member of WTO. Russia is on the verge of becoming a WTO member and we have [laid FTAs] among ourselves. Today, APEC countries are much more integrated and interlinked than they were 15 years ago when APEC was formed, or 10 years ago when Chile first joined.

What benefits does APEC bring to Chile and Latin America?

Chilean Model

How has Chile grown closer to Asia as a member of APEC?

In some ways, there is a real problem of distance between Asia and Latin America. I have attended meetings in Brunei, Shanghai, Bangkok, Kuala Lumpur. I have had to travel 30 hours, stopping in two or three places before I get to my destination. Asia is not our next-door neighbour.

It takes more than 24 hours to reach some of the cities. But with long-range jets, faster planes, direct flights, the distance is getting shorter. With the Internet, telecommunications, the distance between our countries, in some sense, is much shorter today. Chile would like to be the link between Asia and Latin America, since geographically, we are the closest to Asia. What will give us the edge will be not just our FTAs with Asian countries but our connectivity to Asia. We have direct flights to Australia and New Zealand. We are hoping there will be direct flights to Singapore, Hong Kong and Seoul. Just a few years ago, the only way to get to Asia from Chile was through Los Angeles or through Europe. In many ways, in actual distance, Europe is farther away from Chile than Asia but that's how our historical routes developed. We believe we can be a launching pad for Asia as it develops ties with Latin America, and East Asia can be a launching pad as we move further from China to India.

It's not just trade of goods between Latin America and Asia. In Chile, we have placed a lot of emphasis on education, on building our higher education system, on getting graduate student ratios up, and that should help us build a strong services sector. The days when countries relied mainly on manufacturing and agriculture are over. We need to build a strong services sector and, for that, we need a highly educated workforce. We are interested in outsourcing. We are getting financial firms to establish back offices in Chile to serve all Spanish-speaking countries. There is Spain, there is a huge Hispanic community in the US and there are Spanish-speaking countries in Central and South America. But English is now widely spoken in Chile and other Latin American countries. Indeed, English is going to be a topic at the APEC summit. It is becoming the international language of trade. It is important to discuss what we non-English-speaking APEC countries can do to improve the level of English as an essential second language.

In the past, Chile's destiny was linked to North America and, to some ex-tent, Europe. Do you foresee the day when your destiny will be linked to Asia?

Already, you can see our destiny is linked to Asia. Asia is the biggest buyer of our goods. How can we have all our eggs in the American basket when Asia is our biggest trading partner? You look at history. First, it was the Mediterranean region, then it was the North Atlantic — Europe and the US. Now, it's Asia. China is becoming the engine of growth; India is emerging. But that's where our opportunity is: the other side of the Pacific Ocean. We need to find linkages and to see where we can fit in and ride on this Asian boom.

The World Economic Forum and other international organisations have recognised Chile as one of the most competitive economies in Latin America. What makes Chile different in a continent like Latin America, which has lagged behind other regions? How has Chile reformed itself so quickly to become such a competitive economy?

We are a small country that really needs to create jobs and grow faster and, once we realised that to grow we need to have a more globally competitive economy, not one that is closed behind protective walls, we took the challenge to open up our economy and compete with global players. Initially, we suffered. We used to have 170,000 textile workers in Chile. When we opened up, that number was eventually reduced to 30,000. Now, we are globally competitive and the number of textile workers is growing.

We are importing linen because it is produced with subsidies there and we are exporting back fully-stitched clothes and suits to Europe. The Europeans are exporting low-cost raw materials and Chile [is exporting] high-end work. That's how we have increased value-added in our economy, more than we used to in the past.

We also have a strong macroeconomic policy, a growing fiscal surplus, autonomous monetary policy and privatisation. We opened up our highways to be built by private operators, for example. The money we save goes to pay for secondary or rural roads, while the private sector builds the highways or roads in and around big cities like Santiago, or in getting drinkable water to rural areas. Because of all the growth, we can have social cohesion and then start to invest in the future, getting computers for our students, raising standards of higher education, getting more kids into college. Today, seven in 10 university students are first-generation, whose parents never went to university. If we want to compete abroad, we need social cohesion in order to avoid internal social tensions that can result from changes that need to be put in place to build a competitive economy.

The Chilean economy is likely to grow 5.5 per cent this year - one of the fastest in Latin America. This is the fastest the economy has grown since 1997-98. But this high growth is still way behind the 7 per cent or 7.5 per cent at which the economy was growing in the mid-1990s. What structural changes do you think are still necessary to keep the economy growing at a faster pace?

We need to increase the amount of investments to generate higher growth like the 7 per cent or 7.5 per cent that is needed to create sufficient Jobs. What happened in the 1990s was that there were huge new foreign investments, and that kept the pace of growth high. As investments tapered off, growth slowed. Today, the rate of investment is 25 per cent of our gross national product. We need to raise it to 30 per cent or Chile's economy is 35 per cent of GNR in expected to grow order to achieve 5.5 per cent this year, but that, we either need to increase our internal savings or we need new inflows of foreign capital. If copper prices remain high, we are sure there will be huge new investments in the mining area. Our real problem is putting in growth drivers that can create more jobs for our people. We have 9 per cent unemployment. We need to generate 7 per cent or 8 per cent growth; only then can we seriously start to bring down unemployment to more acceptable levels. At 9 per cent, unemployment is still too high and a main source of concern. But that's why we are emphasising services like outsourcing, information technology and higher education.

In recent years, Chile has diversified away from its dependence on commodities like copper. Copper now makes up about 40 per cent of exports, down from 80 per cent. We are spending more on research and development as well as training.

The economy of Chile has done very well in the past year, partly because of demand from the high-growth Asian region — particularly China — for Chile's key commodities like copper. Is the boom from copper exports helping Chile diversify its exports to Asia? Are you likely to see more interest from Asian consumer nations like India and China, which have a huge hunger for commodities, to grow their presence in Chilean mining as well as down stream processing industries?

Copper used to be 80 per cent of our exports; now, it is around 40 per cent. Most of it used to go to North America, Europe and Australia, some of it to Japan. Now it's China, Korea and, soon, it will be India driving up the demand. We are keen to grow our ties with Asia because Asia is important to us. 28 per cent of our exports are to Asia. Only 24 per cent of exports go to the US. Even the 1998 Asian crisis helped Chile. During the crisis, our wine exports to Japan went up 30 per cent or 40 per cent. We found out that it was because Japanese were importing more Chilean wine and less French wine. Aside from copper, wine and salmon are our major exports. We are now the world's second largest exporter of salmon and we are increasing our share of the market. We are also exporting a lot of forestry products, paper and pulp.

There is no tomorrow without yesterday *

IN SANTIAGO CHILE'S President Ricardo Lagos talks to Ibrahim Nafie about healing the wounds of dictatorship and of what it means to be a leftist presiding over a free market economy.

Your leftist government presides over a highly de-regulated, free market economy which is also intensely integrated in the global economy. Would you explain the thinking behind your policy?

The major point is that we are a small country. We are 15 million people and the only way to develop our economy is to use our human resources and to integrate them into the world. This means a tremendous investment in education and in health but it means, also, that we have to compete on the world stage because the domestic market is small.

At the same time our geographical location is rather unusual. Chile, during the 19th and 20th centuries, was something of an island. We have the Andes to our west, desert to the north and the Pacific Ocean.

Where was the centre? The centre used to be the Mediterranean and then after WWII the world stage moved from the Mediterranean to the North Atlantic. The major change in world trade occured with the shift to Europe and the United States. And after that came the emergence of Asia, Japan and today China. Suddenly we discovered that the major growth in world trade is

* *Interview in the weekly magazine Al Ahram, Cairo, Egypt, April 14-20ᵗʰ 2005*

now taking place in the Pacific, for the first time ever. The ocean before us is where world trade is moving and thus, for the first time, we faced the challenge of how we might act as a bridge between the growing Asian economies and Latin America.

That meant that we had to be a part of that world. It was an opportunity, and therefore we opened up. I don't believe in neo-liberal policies. I believe in sound macro-economic management. But that doesn't mean that you are a rightist or left wing. It means that you're doing what you have to do. The difference is that the neo-liberals believe in the market for everything. Well, the market might be good in defining what kind of shoes we are going to have but it is not going to solve problems in areas where goods and services have to be available for everybody. Decisions in that part of the economy must, in a democracy, be made by citizens.

When I say I want 12 years compulsory education, and I introduce that change in Chile, it is because we are in a position to guarantee 12 years of compulsory education for everybody. Or the reforms we have introduced in health, or the provision of drinkable water in rural areas - it is the same. Drinkable water in rural areas is expensive to provide, so it must be provided by the state. We define drinkable water as a good that has to be provided to everybody.

We should understand that the market may be a useful tool in some spheres but in the kind of society that we are building it is the citizen who has the last word. And in a democracy it is the citizen who defines what kind of goods and services are public goods and services, and if they are public then they have to be available to everybody. So that's why I respond, when some say that I seem a bit right-wing given my economic policies, that no, I am not right-wing. We pursue growth so we can also have equity.

We have been able to reduce poverty. 40 per cent of Chileans used to live beneath the poverty line. Now it is 18 per cent, and I hope that by the end of the term of my government [in 2006] the 220,000 families who are currently under the poverty line will no

There is no tomorrow without yesterday

longer be in that situation.

Would you elaborate on some of the lessons learned by the Chilean left from the tragic experience of the Popular Unity government under the late Salvador Allende?

A few moments ago I was on the phone with the widow of Salvador Allende. We are very good friends and she had sent me a message of condolence on the death of my mother and I called her to say thank you.

I think that the main lesson to learn is that if you want to make a profound change in a society you need to have the political backing of a majority in that society. In some cases, in a democracy, you might be able to form a government but without the full backing of the majority. That was the case at the time of Allende. Now we have a broad coalition of Socialists with Christian Democrats - very unusual in European terms - which first defeated General Pinochet in a plebiscite [in 1998, a majority voted no to a new term for Pinochet, opening the way to multi-candidate presidential elections]. Then we discovered that it was essential to have a broad majority to introduce the changes that we've been able to achieve in Chile. That is the lesson. We discovered that because of a broad majority we were able to move forward.

Let me put it another way. At the time of the conflict with Iraq we said no in the Security Council; we said 'no [to the Americans], you need the backing of the world community.' In other words, if you want to make changes that are important, you need the backing of the majority of any society's various sectors. I think that during Allende's time we did not understand that very well. It was also a very different world then, what with the Cold War.

The left is now in government in seven Latin American countries, excluding Cuba. Does Latin America offer a new model in this respect?

I don't think that it is possible to talk of a model. Let me say that this situation is probably the result of policies adopted in much of Latin America during the 1990s. Even though they were able to stimulate growth the policies pursued did not promote equality within these societies. So, when they were talking every day about how their economies were growing; when people saw on TV that there was growth, they didn't see that growth coming into their houses. They did not have better shoes, or better access to education and health, so the sense grew that the policies were flawed. And in a democracy this creates change.

I think what happened in Brazil, Argentina, Venezuela and Uruguay, has a lot to do with that. Ours was the only coalition that was able to stay in power; we started in 1990 and were able to remain in power and we hope that we will continue after my term expires [in 2006] and this, I think, is because we have been able to deliver the other part of the equation.

The differences between the various models in Latin America are striking. If you are living, say, in Brazil, which is huge, almost a continent, with so many millions of people, the market is massive, so instead of opening the economy the first thing they tried to do was to preserve their own market for Brazilians. They have tariffs that are much higher than ours, but this is simply because the realities, the economic realities of the countries are different. We have been able to conclude free trade agreements with the United States and with Europe before Brazil because for us it has been much easier.

For these reasons it is difficult to talk of a Latin American model. Yet all our countries have learned, as the Latin American left has learned, that we need to keep economic accounts in order.

There has been very little retribution for abuses committed under the military dictatorship. How is Chile coming to terms with that dark period in its history?

I think we have been able to advance a lot. There are four major areas of concern: first, with regards to those who were assassinated or who disappeared during the dictatorship. My predecessor President Aylwin appointed a presidential commission, the so-called Truth and Reconciliation Commission, the idea of which was to some extent adopted by our South African friends,

There is no tomorrow without yesterday

which issued a report presented about what happened. This was followed by the provision of compensation to the widows and other family members of the victims.

There were also measures adopted to compensate Chileans forced into exile, with compensation provided to Chileans returning from exile. A third group was made up of those who lost their jobs as a result of being expelled by the junta. Three laws have been passed in parliament already to make amends to such people.

The last aspect in addressing this period is, in my opinion, the most important. I appointed a commission to present a report on what happened to political prisoners under the dictatorship. Thirty-five thousand people testified to the commission. Twenty-eight thousand were registered as people who had been imprisoned, and most of them were tortured. This is probably the most complete report, as far as I know, of what happened under the dictatorship. It was very moving, at times very hard to read because it includes descriptions of the detention centres, and of the kind of torture that was performed in such places. It is a very complete report, and I think that following it's publication Chile was in a much better position to look ahead. That is why I say there is no tomorrow without yesterday.

Let me add that the Presidential Commission which I appointed was headed by a bishop of the Catholic Church, a man who in the old days was able to face up to the dictatorship. The Church in Chile, by the way, played a very important role in defending human rights. And the members of the commission belonged to all political sides in Chile, from the left and the right.

I think it was a very good experience. After the report was issued parliament approved compensation to the victims. But more important is that the tribunals are now working, and many of those who committed human rights abuses are in prison.

Declassified CIA documents revealed to a large degree the extent of US complicity in the military coup in 73, and the abuses that followed it, not only in Chile but across Latin America through Operation Condor. Would you comment?

I think that Operation Condor represented 'state of the art' of dictatorship, if you will allow me to put it that way; for in that operation you had several dictatorships being integrated.

On the other hand, it seems to me that this whole period was rooted in the assumptions of the Cold War. The Cold War justified everything: 'I can do anything to you because you represent evil; you are on the wrong side of history.' Fortunately the Cold War is over, and now we live in a different world. Still, these revelations reveal the kind of excesses that men were capable of committing during that period of history.

How successful have your efforts been to introduce constitutional reforms to deepen democracy and reduce the role of the military in the Chilean state structure?

I would say that we have not been very successful in amending the constitution. We have been much more successful in making our military forces understand that, in today's world, it is only democracy that allows one to walk on this planet.

This morning I received the commander-in-chief of the Turkish armed forces. I was in Turkey recently and I invited him to visit, and this morning he was here, along with the commander-in-chief of the Chilean army. And I would say that they now understand and accept that it is the civilian government that has the right to make decisions about military issues, about defence.

I hope that this year, which will be my last in office, that constitutional amendments will finally be approved. But as regards the military, the constitutional amendments will in effect recognise something that already exists in Chile.

What is Chile's perspective on the architecture of the global economy, and what needs to be done to make it more equitable and humane?

If we are to live in a global world; if globalisation is a fact that we have to face, then we must have rules governing the process. If globalisation is not governed by rules, then rules will be imposed by the those with the greatest power. This is a fact of history. And this is why multilateral institutions are so important for us. This is why the role of the United Nations and other international and regional bodies is so important. It is only through the rules of such bodies that you can have norms governing things such as trade, financial markets and capital flows.

Multilateralism is not only a question of security and peace, it is a necessity for a planet that gets smallerby the day.

Let me give a small example. If you go from Santiago to Punta Arenas in the south of Chile you will find that for children to go out in the sun they have to cover their heads. The ozone layer is so thin over there that not to do so means their skin would burn.

What can I do? Where should I go to protest about gas emissions from the northern hemisphere? I have mentioned this to President Bush. I said to him: 'Mr Bush I understand your position with regards to the Kyoto Protocol, but if it is not Kyoto, I must have some place to go and complain, and to ask now we are going to remedy this.'

In the same way that a national community will define some goods as goods that have to be protected, there are other goods that have to be protected on a global level. Some kind of institutional framework has to be developed to do this. This is new. It did not happen in the past but it is going to happen more and more in the future.

Chile is unique in the number of unilateral and multilateral free trade agreements it has with the outside world. Would you explain this phenomenon?

I have pointed out that as we are a small country we decided to compete on the global market. And we have been able to find some areas in which we can compete effectively. For instance, we export salmon, we export wine and fruit. Of course, we export copper as well.

But more important is that we are now exporting services. We have advanced considerably in the area of information technologies. In Chile today 85 per cent of personal income tax is paid through the Internet. On the Internet you can find what your statement should be according to the Internal Revenue Service. The government will tell you, we believe you are earning such and such, as a way to facilitate the filing of your tax returns. And in doing this we are encouraging small and medium-sized firms to become much more involved in information technology.

What are your views on the stalling of the Free Trade Area Agreement of the Americas, especially given that Chile is already party to such an agreement with the NAFTA countries?

It has been a success for us. We've been able to increase our exports by more than 30 per cent in a single year, so we have no complaints. Nevertheless, the fact that we have such an agreement does not mean that we have solved all the issues concerning trade. For instance, we have been unable to discuss the issue of anti-dumping legislation in the United States, which is going to be discussed at the World Trade Organisation. And over intellectual property rights, we still have some issues to discuss with the United States.

It is easier for us to engage with Europe over agricultural issues because in this area our competition with Europe is not as significant as it is for Brazil and Argentina. But I would still say that the fact that we have such an agreement with Europe does not mean that we have no interest in discussing agriculture at the Doha round. These issues should be dealt with on a multilateral level.

What is Chile's position on the current calls by several countries to re-draw the global political map, emphasising multilateralism and greater democracy in the United Nations system?

Today's institutions represent, to some extent, the world as it existed in 1945. This is why multilateral institutions have to be updated in line with contemporary realities. And I believe that this is what lies behind the report presented by the commission to UN Secretary-General Kofi Annan to be discussed at the next General Assembly. We are looking forward to this discussion.

How does Chile view the forthcoming Arab-South American Summit, and what are your expectations from the Arab side in

There is no tomorrow without yesterday

order to make the summit a success?

When you go back to 1945 and recall the Charter of San Francisco, you find that the Pan- American Union on one side, and the Arab League on the other, played an essential role in shaping the UN system, along with the major world powers, of course.

The forthcoming summit, then, is a revision of what we did some 60 years ago. And I think that in view of the role Egypt is playing in world affairs, and of what we here are trying to do, the time has come to hold this kind of meeting and to discuss, not only on a multilateral but also on a bilateral basis, how our regions can complement one another, and to what extent we have similar views on how the world as a whole should work. And if we are able to do this then I am sure that our common voice is going to be louder and more effective.

My country, as you know, has observer status at the Arab League, and this is a reflection of our understanding of the important role the Arab world plays in world affairs. Our political relations are excellent but our economic ties are lagging behind political relations. This is something I discussed with President Mubarak in Cairo last January.

How would you evaluate the current state of bilateral ties between Chile and Egypt, and what in your view needs to be done to improve them at all levels?

Egypt and Chile have had diplomatic relations since 1929. And during the last two decades, under President Mubarak's leadership, Egypt has been able to modernise substantially. And because we are so open economically we feel that this is a part of the world where there is considerable room for strengthening ties.

We used to be self-sufficient in oil in Chile. Now our oil is depleted. Yet the know-how is still there, and thishas led to successful joint ventures in Egypt in the area of oil exploration and production.

I think that this is the sort of area in which we can work together. Another area in which I believe we could cooperate is agriculture. When I was in Egypt I found some Chilean businessmen investing in production in Egypt aimed at the European market. This kind of mutual investment can be important for both countries. The time has come to bring our economic relations up to the level of our political and diplomatic relations.

The importance of dreaming about the future *

CHILE'S PRESIDENT Ricardo Lagos is considered one of Latin America's most outstanding leaders. After five years in office, his popularity continues to grow. On Monday April 4, he planned to begin a tour of several European countries, starting with Holland, but this was put off at the last minute because of a deterioration in the health of his mother, who is 108 years old.

The government coalition - the Concertación de Partidos por la Democracia - has held office for longer than any other political coalition in Chile's history and everything indicates that it will continue to hold this record in the foreseeable future. Although this is a very promising outlook for the coalition, it could also be very worrying because time erodes founding principles, weakens loyalties and undermines internal discipline. There was a strong ethical and idealistic element in the origins of the Concertación. Where is that element today after 15 years in power?

There was a learning process. Our first challenge - the challenge that brought us together - was to make the transition from authoritarianism, or dictatorship, to democracy. As we made that transition, we began to envisage greater and more difficult challenges: those of becoming a country that is open to the world, of visualising our country's development, and of how, as an open country, we needed to create institutions to increase social cohesion. In other words, how to become a more modern, liberal and free country.

* *Interview by José Zepeda Varas, Director of the Latin American Department of Radio Nederland, The Netherlands, April 4th 2005*

The importance of dreaming about the future

That, I believe, is what has given the Concertación a new role. The issue is no longer dictatorship or democracy; it is how we give democracy social content. We have, therefore, learned that the same force of a great coalition, which was needed to return to democracy, is perhaps also still needed - and more so - to address these other challenges. I believe that is why we have strong support in the country. People perceive that we are leaving behind the dichotomy between dictatorship and democracy and emerging as a country that aspires to become a developed nation within the next few decades.

A political coalition can stay together for different reasons - ideals, the thirst for power, or even out of fear. What keeps the Concertación together?

A vision of the society we want to create, one with greater democracy and higher economic growth, but also with greater social cohesion. And the latter is fundamental because it requires public policies. The market is useful for many things, but it doesn't provide social cohesion. We are all consumers, but we are unequal in our purchasing power, whereas social cohesion is determined by citizens and, as citizens, we are all equal in the votes we cast. Our task as a coalition is, therefore, to ensure that the benefits of growth reach every region of the country, however remote, and each and every segment of society, however remote or humble. And that requires policies that oblige us to discriminate - not, as the market discriminates, on the basis of purchasing power, but on the basis of needs. When we established 12 years of compulsory schooling, what we were doing was transforming education into a public good that does not depend on market forces. We have to guarantee each and every Chilean 12 years of education. And the same applies to our reform of healthcare or to housing. I think it is these social policies that make the difference in the type of country we want to build, and I think this is now understood better than before.

You also hold another record in your country's political history.

The importance of dreaming about the future

You are ending your term of office with an unprecedented level of support, and that is an invaluable political asset. In what way could that asset serve to strengthen the party system and, specifically, the Concertación?

What's happening is, as you say, very interesting - it goes back many years - and it means that many people identify with the coalition, rather than with the individual parties that form part of it. When we founded the Concertación - the Socialists, the Radicals, the members of the Party for Democracy and the Christian Democrats - we formed a great conglomerate, but each of us participated in it by representing our own sector. However, young people today - of, say, 20 or 25 - cannot remember any other government but the Concertación and I couldn't say that they identify first with one of the parties and only then with the coalition. I think it's rather the other way around. First, they identify with the coalition and only then perhaps look to see whether any party or sector represents them better than another. And some people simply describe themselves as independents who support the Concertación. Now that is a challenge. And, of course, if we have such significant public support, it's also a challenge to ensure that we do our job efficiently so we don't disappoint our supporters.

And there's a very important difference here: a government comes to an end, but its political parties continue to exist. In democracy, a government has a set period of office, but a coalition has a duty to continue dreaming beyond its period of office. In that sense, the Concertación has been capable of setting new challenges under each of its leaders - first, President Aylwin, then President Frei, and now myself. And I am sure the next election will produce a leadership that will also embody the new dreams of the Concertación.

Former President Aylwin, in the historic context in which he governed, coined a phrase that, at the time, seemed sensible - "justice to the extent that it is possible". The "unimaginable" progress that Chile has achieved on human rights and, specifically, as regards the access of society to the truth, suggests that,

The importance of dreaming about the future

today, justice as far as is possible, means justice without limits. Do you think the task of building Chile's future still requires concessions as regards the full exercise of justice?

No. I don't think so. We have made sufficient progress in this field. "There is no future without a past; we cannot build the future while we are still hiding yesterday's tragedies under the carpet." I think Chile has done something in this field that is pretty much without precedent. I asked a group of highly respected people to prepare a report on political detention and torture in Chile and that has allowed all Chileans to glimpse the tragedy of what happened to our country. Thirty-five thousand people testified before the Commission and 28,000 of those testimonies were verified to its satisfaction. And the State, as well as asking for the forgiveness of those victims, is seeking - if only quite modestly - to repair part of the harm they suffered and is offering them pensions for the rest of their lives. That is part of the progress we have achieved. At the same time, the law courts are doing their job. There are few countries in the world where former members of a secret police are serving long prison sentences. We have shown that no-one is above the law, or beyond its reach. And all this has happened in a country that has continued to go about its daily life normal.

I think, therefore, that we are close to being able to say: Yes, it's true, there is no future without a past, and we have no fear of looking at what happened and of punishing what needs to be punished.

Before we leave domestic issues, perhaps we can look at the case of the two women presidential candidates - not at whether one or the other will take the nomination, but at the important issue of whether this is just a coincidence or whether it reflects a deeper change in the role of women in Chile's national life.

It's a reflection of a much deeper change because, in this period, we've also seen the first woman - two, in fact - presiding over the Chamber of Deputies, the first women reaching the Supreme Court and the first women qualifying with top marks as fighter

The importance of dreaming about the future

pilots in the Air Force. And, even more noticeably, we have women presiding over trade unions in the copper industry, a mining activity. However, what is even more important is that, over the last 15 years, the participation of women in the labour force has increased from 30% to 38%. We still have a long way to go to reach European standards, but I think it's a trend that is here to stay, and perhaps the best indication of the fact that it represents a deep cultural change, is that in today's Chile no one asks, "Hey, but do you think a woman can really be President?" If that is not a topic of our daily conversations, it's because Chileans see the idea of a woman as President as something normal. It's true that one of the candidates was the first woman Defence Minister and the other was the first woman Foreign Minister (the first woman to form part of a Cabinet in Chile was Justice Minister Adriana Olguín de Baltra in 1950). But, beyond that, I think it's also important that these profound cultural changes have not been confined to the participation of women, but also include the elimination of film censorship, greater press freedom, the abolition of the death penalty, a reform of family law and the legalisation of divorce, and also a revitalisation of our country's cultural life. In 2004, 15% of those people who went to the cinema did so to see a Chilean film. Chile has changed and that's reflected in this cultural renaissance.

Let's move to international issues. Why has your government put so much effort into a Chilean becoming the Secretary General of the Organisation of American States? I understand, like the rest of Latin America, that new hemispheric relations are desirable, but are they possible?

The basis for a country's foreign policy is the geographic region in which it is located. In our case, that is Latin America, but also the wider region of the Americas which, of course, includes the United States and Canada. So, if the OAS, the Organisation of American States, is the voice of the Americas, the question is how we can make it a place in which the real and weighty issues of the world are debated. We see that these can range from agreements

The importance of dreaming about the future

or disagreements as regards the members of the United Nations Security Council to how we should address the matter of international trade or the great issues that occupy the multilateral agenda, either to define our differences or to reach agreements. When the United States, which is the world's super power, has important issues to discuss, it goes to Europe and talks about them in NATO or with the European Union. Or it talks about them with the Asian countries in ASEAN. My question is why it can't discuss them directly with us. Our view is that the Organisation of American States needs to be a proper debating forum, in which we look each other in the eye and set out our positions. It fell to Chile to be a member of the UN Security Council during the crisis over the Iraq war and we were in daily telephone contact with all the leaders. Wouldn't it have been more logical to have got together around a table - and this is something I have discussed with President George Bush - to listen to each others' opinions? Perhaps we wouldn't have reached an agreement, but we would have had a much clearer picture of what was really happening.

That is why we believe that, in the Organisation of American States, we should take a leap forward. And that belief was reflected in Chile's decision to put forward one of its most respected political figures, who is extremely well qualified to undertake such a task.

As regards the change in international relations and Latin America specifically, I'd like to raise two issues - that of Peru and of Bolivia. In the crisis triggered by Chile's sales of arms in the case of Peru and Ecuador, Chilean government officials have given assurances that the issue was dealt with 10 years ago. If that is so, why has it acquired its present dimension?

It's difficult to analyse the causes, but it's true that this issue was raised 10 years ago at the time of the conflict between Peru and Ecuador. Chile gave the Peruvian government all the information it had and, as a result, went on to act normally as a guarantor in accordance with the 1942 Treaty, which established the countries that would serve in this role in the case of a conflict between

The importance of dreaming about the future

Ecuador and Peru. Peru thanked Chile for the role it played and we understood that the issue had been totally settled. It was the declarations of an Ecuadorean general, on which he subsequently backed down, that triggered this situation. We hope it can be dealt with through the agreed channels. With Peru, as with Argentina, we have what we call a "2+2 arrangement" and Chile's Defence and Foreign Ministers will meet Peru's Foreign and Defence Ministers on April 21 when I hope the issue will be resolved.

Mr. President, Bolivia's request for access to the sea has surely never had greater international support than at present, at least in the speeches that we hear. But, apart from that, is a solution possible given that the two countries have not had diplomatic relations for a very long time?

The first thing I would say is that it is regrettable that we do not have diplomatic relations. That is why Chile has always said that it believes they should be re-established. Apart from this - and it is Bolivia's sovereign decision whether it has relations with Chile or not - we have also expressed our willingness to comply with all the requests of our Bolivian friends in such a way that their country's development is not impeded by its lack of a sea coast. That is why we have also offered all manner of facilities for the export of Bolivian gas. However, I would like to point out that it is complicated to re-open a debate about the terms of a treaty. What would happen to Europe if it started to review all the treaties that have affected its frontiers over the last 150 years? It's difficult to imagine.

Moreover, in the specific case of Bolivia, it's true that it started life as a country with an area of 2,200,000 km^2 and that, today, it has 1,000,000. Out of the 1,200,000 km2 that Bolivia has lost, 110,000 km2 went to Chile as a result of the war of 1879. In other words, the vast majority of the territory that Bolivia has lost has to do with conflicts with other countries, not with Chile.

But, whatever the case, it's obviously difficult to ask Chile to divide its country in two in order to provide Bolivia with a sovereign corridor. No country can do that. So the only possibility is a corridor alongside Chile's northern frontier with Peru but, in that case, under an agreement that Chile has with Peru, Peru would have to acquiesce. As a result, I have often thought that, whatever shape this issue takes in the future, the key to Bolivia's access to the sea is really held by Peru, rather than Chile.

You are about to begin a tour of a number of European countries. The European Union has a couple of trade agreements with Latin American countries, but there is a critical view which maintains that relations are poor and are passing through a not very promising period. Will it be possible, in the foreseeable future, to revitalise relations with Europe?

First of all, I would like to point out that Chile has an agreement with Europe that not only covers trade, but also includes an agreement on cooperation and a political agreement. Europe continues to be the main market for our exports and, therefore, unlike other Latin American countries, Chile's trade is very diversified - 30% to Europe, 25% to Asia, 20% to the United States and Canada. As a result, Europe is a very important partner for us.

Secondly, I believe that Europe is more important to us because it reflects a capacity to combine economic growth with very clear social policies. There is a tendency towards greater social cohesion in Europe, towards a society that works in a more appropriate way and, in that sense, we have a great deal to learn from Europe.

With the end of the Cold War, Europe discovered the East European countries and what mattered for a long time was what a Dutch banker once told me during a visit to Chile - "you'll understand that to get to Chile, I have to spend 16 hours on a plane whereas I can get to Poland in 2 hours so I think that, in the coming years, we're going to be spending more time in Warsaw than in Santiago". But that stage is over now. Most of those countries have now been incorporated into Europe and, as a result, the time has come to look at other parts of the world. Meanwhile, Latin America has grown and there has been a consolidation of democracy. That has brought a new vision of relations between Latin America and Europe and, in this new stage of relations,

The importance of dreaming about the future

Chile is prepared to play an active role.

From my point of view, the other important issue is that when Europe thinks of the Third World and of developing countries, its mind often goes immediately to Africa. I understand that, but I think it would be a grave mistake to assume that there is a sort of vertical division of the world in which Latin America falls within the sphere of the United States, and Africa in the sphere of Europe, etc. That seems to me an over-simplification. And there is another factor that is not insignificant - what countries like Chile owe to the European countries and, particularly, to Holland. When the situation here was so difficult and complex, when human rights were not respected, Holland played such a decisive role in so many institutions that helped to maintain free thought about Chile and to support the NGOs that were fighting for respect for human rights. I think this created very strong ties with Europe and I am sure that, in a democratic system, these ties can only become closer still.

To conclude, I'd like to return to Chile. Mr. President, what explains the country's success, not only politically but also economically and socially? In a region that has so many needs, isn't it grounds for jealousy and envy?

Chile dared to seek international integration, to compete in the world and to open the country to the world - something similar to what a country like Holland did. Holland is also a country with a small market and it dared to insert itself into Europe and to look out into the rest of the world. And it did so much earlier, with the Dutch sailors who opened up new navigation routes and the India Company and so on. In other words, faced with their small size - which is difficult to change - our countries opted to become societies that compete in the world. That has many implications and requires many prior definitions. That is what Chile has been doing. What is referred to as "Chile's success" is, I would say, mostly a case of reaching agreement among all Chileans as to the type of development we want. The key lies in not letting any Chilean fall behind and that calls for very active social policies.

The importance of dreaming about the future

And, well, if we can stick to that course, we may, in the future, achieve better development even than our European friends. And, of course, I also believe that the other Latin American countries are increasingly beginning to look in the same direction.

Place Index

African Union 133
Argentina 30, 74, 76, 153, 168, 171, 172,140,141, 180, 183, 190, 192, 197, 218
Asunción 140
Australia 201, 205, 206
Asia 138, 145
Balkans 118
Bali 15
Bangkok 138
Bering Strait 101,
Brazil 10, 30, 74, 76, 153,160,140,141, 180, 183, 190, 192, 214, 218,
Bolivia 190, 226, 227
Bonn 167
Bordeaux 154
Boston 49
Bretton Woods 19, 96, 116, 123, 170
Brunei 30, 207
Burma 109, 110
Cairo 219
Canada 74, 123, 139, 193, 195, 201, 204, 225, 228
Cancún 77
Cape Horn 101, 135
Cape of Good Hope 135
Caribbean 66, 124
Chapel Hill 172
Chechnya 118
Chile 9, 10, 11, 12, 13, 14, 16, 17, 18, 19, 22, 23, 24, 25, 26, 28, 29, 30, 31, 33, 34, 35, 36, 37, 38, 39, 40, 41, 42, 45, 46, 47, 48, 59, 60, 71, 72, 73, 74, 75, 76, 78, 79, 80, 91, 103, 105, 116, 117, 121, 124, 129, 130, 131, 133, 134, 135, 137, 138, 139, 140, 141, 143, 144, 145, 149, 150, 151, 152, 153, 154, 155, 156, 157, 159, 161, 162, 163, 165, 169, 173, 174, 175, 177, 178, 179, 180, 181, 182, 183, 184, 185, 186, 189, 190, 191, 192, 193, 194, 195, 196, 197, 198, 199,

Place Index

201, 203, 204, 206, 208, 209, 210, 211, 212, 213, 215, 216, 219, 224, 225, 228, 229
China 30, 137, 138, 139, 141, 204, 206, 211
Copenhagen 9
Cuba 100
Doha 56
Durban 134
Ecuador 162, 226, 227
Egypt 219, 220
England 80, 156,162, 170
Falkland Islands 153
France 30, 165, 166, 170, 180, 200
Germany 40, 154, 166, 167, 200
Guayaquil 185
Haiti 18
Hiroshima 40, 165
Holland 221, 229
Hong Kong 56, 168
Italy 40, 154
India 30, 143, 144, 145, 207, 210
Iraq 18, 70, 78, 96, 97, 125, 198, 199, 200
Jamaica 124
Japan 30, 40, 77, 139, 141,160,163, 165, 178, 205, 211
Korea 130,139, 141
Kyoto 17, 44, 217
Los Angeles 207
Madrid 15, 65, 66, 167
Malaysia 139, 162
México 74, 77, 79 124, 139,168, 190, 193, 195, 198, 201, 204, 205
Montevideo 140
Moscow 151
Myanmar 109
Nagasaki 40, 165
New Zealand 30, 201, 205, 206
New York 15, 134, 154, 168
Nice 79
Norway 197

Place Index

North Carolina's 203
Ouro Prieto 141
Paraguay 180, 190
Paris 43, 107, 154, 162, 163
Peru 139, 190, 206, 226, 227, 228
Persian Gulf 185
Punta Arenas 17, 217
Poland 228
Rio Bravo 101
Rio de Janeiro 9, 65
Rome 154
Russia 139, 165, 168, 183, 200, 206
Rwanda 118
San Francisco 19, 125, 165, 219
Santiago 56, 150, 161, 163, 203, 209, 211, 217, 228
Seattle 13, 83, 166, 170
Seoul 56, 57
Shanghai 207
Singapore 30, 201, 207
South Africa 117, 133, 134, 135
South Korea 30, 74, 129, 195, 204, 205
South America 134, 137, 139, 140, 143
Soviet Union 100, 152, 165
Spain 65, 67, 79, 207
Stockholm 154
Sweden 118
Switzerland 10
Thailand 139
US, United States of America 49, 74, 77, 100, 102, 104, 115, 116, 123, 124, 129, 130, 131, 139, 152, 154, 155, 160, 163, 165, 169, 170, 178, 180, 186, 193, 194, 195, 196, 197, 198, 199, 200, 201, 211, 214, 218, 225, 226, 228, 229
Turkey 168, 183, 216
UK, United Kingdom 70, 79, 200
Uruguay 180
Vietnam 139,
Warsaw 53, 57
Washington 15, 71, 74, 134, 154, 194

Personality Index

Al-Qays, Imru 95
Alessandri, President Jorge 150
Alfonsín, President Raúl 153
Allen, Woody 46
Allende, Presidente Salvador 60, 61, 150, 151, 155, 177, 213,
Almodóvar, Pedro 46
Annan, Kofi 218
Aylwin, President Patricio 27, 130,174, 214, 223
Bergman, Igmar 46
Bertolucci, Bernardo 46
Blair, Prime Minister Tony 72, 78, 80, 198
Blix, Hans 199
Bush, President George 198, 199, 226
Bush, President George W. 165
Bobbio, Norberto 54, 97
Carter, President Jimmy 166
Cardoso, President Fernando 159
Castells, Manuel 40
Chirac, President Jacques 199
Chretien, Prime Minister Jean 121
Churchill,Prime Minister Sir Winston 152
Clinton, President Bill 121, 122, 124
Cochrane, Lord Thomas 79
Coetzee, John 135
De Klerk President Frederik 136
Echavarría, José Medina 37, 38
Egan, Louis 177
Fajnzylber, Fernando 38
Fox, President Vicente 198, 201
Frei, President Eduardo 130, 223
Frei Montalva, President Eduardo 27, 150
Friedman, Milton 151, 152
Fuentes, Carlos 45
Gates, Bill 158, 179

Personality Index

Giscard d´Estaing, President Valery 166
Gordimer, Nadine 135
González, President Felipe 167, 169
Hobsbawm, Eric 9, 96
Hussein, Saddam 198,
Insulza, José Miguel 30,
Jefferson, Thomas 56,
Jintao, President Hu
Kemp, Jack 196
Keynes, John Maynard 70, 78, 170, 175
Lamy, Pascal 121
Lula , President Luiz Inacio 30
Mandela, President Nelson 135, 136
Marín, Gladys 46
Marx, Karl 158
Mbeki, President Tabo 117, 133
Menem, President Carlos 153
Mistral, Gabriela 29, 135
Mitterrand, President François 155
Monnet, Jean 92
Mubarak, President Hosni 219
Nasser, Gamal Abdel 38
Nehru, Prime Minister Jawaharlal 38
Neruda, Pablo 29, 135
O´Higgins, General Bernardo 79, 80
Olguín, Adriana 225
Paz, Octavio 45
Persson, Göran 117
Pinochet, General Augusto 151, 152, 154, 155, 172, 173, 174, 181, 182, 186
Pinto, Aníbal 24
Piñar, Blas
Pöhl, Karl Otto 167
Prats, Carlos
Rammell, Bill
Ricoeur, Paul 106
Rodríguez Zapatero, Prime Minister José Luis 30
Rostow, Walt

Personality Index

Roosevelt, President Franklin Delano, 104, 108
Santa Cruz, Hernán 134
Schmidt, Chancellor Helmut 166
Schroeder, Chancellor Gerhard 30, 70, 75
Schuman, Robert 92
Scorsese, Martin 46
Smith, Geri 177
Suu Kyi, Aung San 109, 110
Thatcher, Prime Minister Margaret 156
Tito, President Josip Broz 38
Valech, Sergio 27
Valdés, Gabriel 173
White, Harry Dexter 78, 170

Acronyms Index

APEC, Asia-Pacific Economic Co-operation
ASEAN, Association of Southeast Asian Nations
CEPAL, Comisión Económica para Latinoamérica y el Caribe (Economic Comission for Latin America and the Caribbean)
CIA, Central Intelligence Agency
CODELCO, Corporación del Cobre (Copper Corporation)
ECLAC, Economic Commission for Latin America and the Caribbean
EFTA, European Free Trade Association
ENAP Empresa Nacional del Petróleo (Oil National Company)
EU, European Union
FDR, Franklin Delano Roosevelt
FTA, Free Trade Agreement
GDP, Gross Domestic Product
GNP, Gross National Product
IDB, Inter-American Development Bank
IMF, International Monetary Fund
MERCOSUR, Mercado Común del Sur (Southern Common Market)
NAFTA, Free Trade Area Agreement of the Americas
NGO, Non-Governmental Organisation
NLD, National League for Democracy (Burma)
OAS, Organisation of American States
OAU, Organisation of African Unity
PTA, Preferential Trade Agreement
UN (United Nations)
WTO (World Trade Organisation)